The Gospel in
Gerard Manley Hopkins

"By the Gate of the Sacred," portrait of Gerard Manley Hopkins,
woodcut by Robert McGovern

The Gospel in Gerard Manley Hopkins

Selections from His Poems, Letters,
Journals, and Spiritual Writings

Edited by Margaret R. Ellsberg
Foreword by Dana Gioia

Plough

Published by Plough Publishing House
Walden, New York
Robertsbridge, England
Elsmore, Australia
www.plough.com

Plough produces books, a quarterly magazine, and Plough.com to encourage people and help them put their faith into action. We believe Jesus can transform the world and that his teachings and example apply to all aspects of life. At the same time, we seek common ground with all people regardless of their creed.

Plough is the publishing house of the Bruderhof, an international Christian community. The Bruderhof is a fellowship of families and singles practicing radical discipleship in the spirit of the first church in Jerusalem (Acts 2 and 4). Members devote their entire lives to serving God, one another, and their neighbors, renouncing private property and sharing everything. To learn more about the Bruderhof's faith, history, and daily life, see Bruderhof.com. (Views expressed by Plough authors are their own and do not necessarily reflect the position of the Bruderhof.)

ISBN: 978-0-87486-822-7
21 20 19 18 17   1 2 3 4 5 6 7

Cover portrait detail by Robert McGovern.

Illustrations by Gerard Manley Hopkins courtesy of the Harry Ransom Center, The University of Texas at Austin.

A catalog record for this book is available from the British Library
Library of Congress Cataloging-in-Publication Data
Names: Hopkins, Gerard Manley, 1844-1889, author. | Ellsberg, Margaret R., editor. | Gioia, Dana, writer of foreword.
Title: The Gospel in Gerard Manley Hopkins : selections from his poems, letters, journals, and spiritual writings / edited by Margaret R. Ellsberg; foreword by Dana Gioia.
Description: Walden, New York : Plough Publishing House, 2017. | Includes bibliographical references.
Identifiers: LCCN 2016057697 (print) | LCCN 2017001404 (ebook) | ISBN 9780874868227 (pbk.) | ISBN 9780874860184 (epub) | ISBN 9780874860191 (mobi) | ISBN 9780874860252 (pdf)
Subjects: LCSH: Christian literature, English. | Catholic Church--In literature.
Classification: LCC PR4803.H44 A6 2017 (print) | LCC PR4803.H44 (ebook) | DDC 828/.809--dc23
LC record available at https://lccn.loc.gov/2016057697

Printed in the United States of America

In memory of Mary Frances Dunham, 1954–2015

✝

Spring

(unfolding rhythm, with sprung leadings: no coun-
terpoint)

: Nothing is so beautiful as Spring —
When weeds, in wheels, shoot long and lovely and lush;
: Thrush's eggs look little low heavens, and thrush
Through the echoing timber does so rinse and wring

: The ear, it strikes like lightnings to hear him sing;
The glassy peartree leaves and blooms, they brush
The descending blue; that blue is all in a rush
Of richness; the racing lambs too have fair their fling.

: What is all this juice and all this joy?
A strain of the earth's sweet being in the beginning
In Eden garden. — Have, get, before it cloy,

Before it cloud, Christ, lord, and sour with sinning,
: Innocent-minded Mayday in girl and boy,
Most, O maid's child, thy choice and worthy the win-
ning.

May 1877

Contents

Foreword

GERARD MANLEY HOPKINS is a singular figure in English-language literature. No other poet has achieved such major impact with so small a body of writing. His mature work consists of only forty-nine poems – none of which he saw published in his lifetime. Even when one adds the two dozen early poems written at Oxford and various fragments found in notebooks after his death, his literary *oeuvre* is meager in size, even for a writer who died in his forties.

Yet Hopkins occupies a disproportionally large and influential place in literary history. Invisible in his own lifetime, he now stands as a major poetic innovator who, like Walt Whitman and Emily Dickinson, prefigured the Modernist revolution. A Victorian by chronology, Hopkins belongs by sensibility to the twentieth century – an impression strengthened by the odd fact that his poetry was not published until 1918, twenty-nine years after his death. This posthumous legacy changed the course of modern poetry by influencing some of the leading poets, including W. H. Auden, Dylan Thomas, Robert Lowell, John Berryman, Geoffrey Hill, and Seamus Heaney.

As W. H. Gardner and N. H. MacKenzie observed in the fourth edition of *The Poems of Gerard Manley Hopkins* (1970), "The steady growth and consolidation of the fame of Gerard Manley Hopkins has now reached a point from which, it would seem, there can be no permanent regression." There is a mixture of relief and wonder in their statement. No one would have predicted the poet's exalted position when the first edition was published, not even its editor, Robert Bridges, who spent much of his introduction apologizing for the poet's eccentricities and obscurities. Hopkins currently ranks as one of the most frequently reprinted poets in English. According to William Harmon's statistical survey of existing anthologies and textbooks, *The Top 500 Poems* (1992), Hopkins stood in seventh place among English-language poets – surpassed only by Shakespeare, Donne, Blake, Dickinson, Yeats, and Wordsworth (all prolific and longer-lived writers). His poetry is universally taught and has inspired a mountain of scholarly commentary. Despite the difficulty of his style, he is also popular among students.

Hopkins is one of the great Christian poets of the modern era. His verse is profoundly, indeed almost totally, religious in subject and nature. A devout and orthodox convert to Catholicism who became a Jesuit priest, he considered poetry a spiritual distraction unless it could serve the faith. This quality makes his popularity in our increasingly secular and anti-religious age seem paradoxical. Yet the devotional nature of his work may actually be responsible for his continuing readership. Hopkins's passionate faith may provide something not easily found elsewhere on the current curriculum – serious and disciplined Christian spirituality.

The history of English poetry is inextricably linked to Christianity. As Donald Davie commented in his introduction to *The New Oxford Book of Christian Verse* (1981), "Through most of the centuries when English verse has been written, virtually all of the writers of that verse quite properly and earnestly regarded themselves as Christian." Not all poetry was explicitly religious, but Christian beliefs and perspectives shaped its imaginative and moral vision. The tradition of explicitly religious poetry, however, was both huge and continuous. Starting with Chaucer, Langland, and the anonymous medieval authors of *The Pearl* and *Sir Gawain and the Green Knight,* religious poetry flourishes for half a millennium. The tradition continues robustly through Donne, Herbert, Vaughan, Traherne, Cowper, Milton, Blake, Wordsworth, Tennyson, both Brownings, and Christina Rossetti – as well the hymnodists Watts, Cowper, and Wesley. Then in the middle of the Victorian era it founders. Matthew Arnold's melancholy masterpiece of anguished Victorian agnosticism, "Stanzas from the Grande Chartreuse" (1855) exemplifies the crisis of faith. Entering the ancient Alpine monastery, Arnold contrasts the millennium of faith it represents with his own unsatisfying rationalism. Arnold articulates his intellectual and existential dilemma: "Wandering between two worlds, one dead, / The other powerless to be born."

Not coincidentally, it was during that moment of growing religious skepticism and spiritual anxiety that Hopkins appeared to transform and renew the tradition of Christian poetry. Consequently, he occupies a strangely influential position in the history of English-language Christian poetry. His audaciously original style not only swept away the soft and sentimental conventions of nineteenth-century religious verse, it also provided a vehicle strong enough to communicate the overwhelming power of his faith. His small body of work – hidden for years – provided most of the elements out of which modern Christian poetry would be born.

PEGGY ELLSBERG'S *The Gospel in Gerard Manley Hopkins* focuses on the central mystery of the author's singularly odd career – how a talented minor Victorian poet suddenly emerged after seven years of silence as a convulsively original master of English verse. For Ellsberg, Hopkins's conversion to Catholicism was the catalytic force, intensified by Jesuit spiritual discipline and intense theological study. Hopkins's poetic formation, she contends, was inextricable from his priestly formation. It was no coincidence that the great explosion of his literary talent occurred as he approached ordination. His conversion had initiated an intellectual and imaginative transformation – initially invisible in the secret realms of his inner life – that produced a new poet embodied in the new priest. For both the man and the writer, the transformation was sacramental.

Although Holy Orders plays a critical role in the chronology of Hopkins's transformation, the connections between his Catholicism and creativity do not end there. The author's religious and imaginative conversion, Ellsberg demonstrates, depended on his vision of all the sacraments, especially the Eucharist. "For him," Ellsberg formulates persuasively, "a consecration made from human language reversed existential randomness and estrangement." Hopkins's belief in transubstantiation and real presence saved him from the painful theological doubts and sentimental spiritual hungers of his Anglican contemporaries; their crepuscular nostalgia and vague longing were replaced by his dazzling raptures of light-filled grace. A brave new world filled his senses with the sacramental energy of creation where every bird, tree, branch, and blossom trembled with divine immanence.

From the start Hopkins's literary champions have been puzzled, skeptical, confused, or even hostile toward his conversion. Catholicism was seen, even by Robert Bridges, as an intellectual impediment that the poet's native genius somehow overcame, though not without liability. Or Hopkins's theology was a cerebral eccentricity that generated an equally eccentric literary style. Ellsberg refutes these condescending views of the poet and the Church. She pays a great poet the respect of taking his core beliefs seriously, not in the least because they have also been both the animating ideas of European civilization and the foundational dogmas of the Roman Catholic Church, which have inspired artists for two millennia.

The Gospel in Gerard Manley Hopkins combines scholarly accuracy with critical acumen. Ellsberg's extensive commentary on Hopkins's verse and prose texts both elucidates his thought and provides illuminating context for the poems. Meanwhile she sustains her larger argument on the spiritual development of the author as a model Christian life of consecration, contemplation, sacrifice, and indeed sanctity. In restoring the focus on the centrality of Hopkins's faith, Ellsberg does not simply clarify the underlying unity of his life and work. She also restores a great poet and modern saint to us, his readers.

Dana Gioia
Poet Laureate of California

PART I

Manor House, Shanklin.
Finished Sept. 21. 1863.

Incompatible Excellences

AN INTRODUCTION

IN THE CATHOLIC CEMETERY called Glasnevin in Dublin, the Jesuit Father Hopkins was buried near Maud Gonne in the summer of 1889. A century later, in 1989, the gravekeeper at Glasnevin referred to the famous priest and poet as "the convert." Although geographically he did not die far from the place of his birth, Gerard Manley Hopkins had traversed vast theological paradigms, revolutionized poetic language, and called down the thunder and lightning of God onto the written page.

Only after leaving the Anglican Church, to which his family was so bound, leaving Oxford University, where he was on track to spend his life, and entering the Jesuit order, known for its insistence on quasi-cadaver-level obedience, did Hopkins boldly take on the visceral Anglo-Saxon two-beat foot that runs through English speech, mix it prodigally with Welsh and Latin and French, mold his lines to Greek forms, and concoct stanza after stanza and sestet after octet of nerve-shocking genius. Arbitrary, stray, he innovated rhythmic power in his poetry. He cut sonnets at ten lines. He flatly rejected everyone's attempts to correct him. His opinions and practices were stubborn to the verge of arrogance and compulsion; in other words, he was coherent. He did as he wished while cloaked in a mantle of obedience. The reader who arrives at the on-ramp to one of Gerard Manley Hopkins's masterpiece poems, or one of his letters or sermons or journal entries, will become the larger for having entered there.

As a Jesuit novice, age twenty-four, Hopkins made a Long Retreat with the extremely important manual called *The Spiritual Exercises of St. Ignatius Loyola,* composed by the Spanish/ Basque priest Ignatius of Loyola in 1522–24, while the Lutheran Reformation simmered in the background. The *Exercises* provide essential guidance for Jesuits (and for anyone interested in directed contemplation). Hopkins would use the *Exercises* for the rest of his life. Perhaps the most influential moment in the *Exercises* occurs when the retreatant is invited to employ *"compositio loci,"* composition of place. Here the text instructs the person in prayer to visualize precisely and in naturalistic detail scenes from the life of Christ. Louis L. Martz, in *The Poetry of Meditation* (1976), characterizes "the composition of place" as essential in the religious poetry of seventeenth-century England. In Hopkins, this exercise influenced his sermons profoundly, and produced potential poetry.

Six months before he died, while on retreat at St. Stanislaus College in Tullabeg, the Jesuit novice-house in Ireland, Hopkins composed his most self-revealing material in his notes on Ignatius's "First Principle." St. Ignatius, founder of the Jesuit order, opened his manual of exercises with the line *"homo creatus est laudare"* – man is created to praise. These words had permanently affected Hopkins. They showed up in his incessant search for creative pattern that made his art form into an homage to the author of all form. Humphry House, early editor of Hopkins's notebooks, wrote:

> No single sentence better explains the motives and direction of Hopkins's life than this: "Man is created to praise." He believed

it as wholly as a man can believe anything; and when regret or sorrow over anything in [Hopkins'] life comes to a critic's mind, this must be remembered. [1]

The specific instruction of the Jesuit *Exercises* clearly influenced the rigorous forms Hopkins chose for his poetry.

Gerard Manley Hopkins employed a sort of religious Expressionism, one certain of the divine and receptive to idiosyncrasy. Yet anthologies necessarily classify him as Victorian, since his short life spanned 1844–89. The Victorian period, 1837–1901, was the great age of teapots, three-volume novels, and piano legs wearing skirts. The Victorian sun never set on the Union Jack, and one out of three inhabitants of the planet was a British subject. Conventional style was heavy – windows hung with dark drapes, parlors densely ornamented. Women wore lace cuffs and men wore stiff collars. The short, stout Queen, ruling the empire with unfailing dignity for six and a half decades, raised terrier dogs. She bore eleven children. She oversaw such events as the Crystal Palace Exhibition in 1851, the Crimean War, and the controversy over Darwin. She slept every night for twenty-five years with a copy of Tennyson's "In Memoriam" under her pillow.

Into the cream of this quirky age, Gerard Hopkins was born. Appropriately eccentric, a firstborn son, surrounded by gifted people, he was destined for success as a wealthy Anglican. His biographers have characterized him as frail, pale, anemic, short (5'2"), thin, too tired to wake up in the mornings, unpunctual, and inclined to wear little girls' slippers with ankle straps. One anti-hagiographical critic claimed that his high-pitched voice conveyed the powerful stereotype of an affluent Englishman, and that his arched eyebrows and long nose conferred on him the appearance of a cartoon snob. A fellow Jesuit described him as "effeminate, with mouse-colored hair." Saying Mass, he was apparently slow and scrupulous, jerking nervously at the slightest noise. When he taught school, the boys described his lessons as bearing "little marketable value." He once foolishly told a group of high school boys that he regretted that he had never seen a naked woman.

But he was also independent and willful, wiry and athletic: his brother Cyril wrote of Gerard's boyhood activities, "He was a fearless climber of trees and would go up in the lofty elm tree standing in our garden . . . to the alarm of onlookers like myself." [2] At Highgate School, he fought stubbornly with his headmaster, Mr. Dyne. Hopkins, age seventeen, wrote in a letter to Charles Luxmoore, "Dyne and I had a terrific altercation. I was driven out of patience and cheeked him wildly and he blazed into me with his riding whip." [3]

As a mature but unpublished poet, he refused to revise a single line of his work, calling his verses "grubs in amber." He possessed unshakable certainties. In brief, he actually was equipped for success – born with numerous silver spoons in his mouth, academically accomplished, artistically sensitive, stoic in the English way. So how could a man who claimed that "the holding of himself back . . . is the root of all moral good" embody such creative fertility that he set a new table for poetry forever? Because of this obscure Victorian Jesuit, the subsequent century produced an enlarged and liberated poetry, including lines like these:

Never until the mankind making
Bird beast and flower
Fathering and all humbling darkness
Tells with silence the last light breaking

Dylan Thomas, from "A Refusal to Mourn the Death, by Fire, of a Child in London"

Hopkins's conversion at age twenty-two to Roman Catholicism notoriously and quite entirely derailed any hope of secular success. He went straight from a Double First at Oxford to incompetently teaching grammar school in the industrial city of Birmingham. In 1868, he capped his apparent folly by entering the Jesuits. A fellow Jesuit wrote, "I have rarely known anyone who sacrificed so much in taking the yoke of religion."[4] When he decided on a religious vocation, he destroyed the sentimental and anxious poems he had written before age twenty-three. The next time he acted as a serious poet, at age thirty-one, having filtered and brewed a fresh poetic, he unleashed the power of nuclear fission in "The Wreck of the Deutschland."

He had burned his early poems – he referred to this moment as his "slaughter of the innocents" – and by the time he wrote "The Wreck," he was an experienced Catholic. He had already claimed that he became a Catholic because "two plus two makes four"; but also, and the poems of the 1870s demonstrate this, he said that he had converted because of the Roman Catholic doctrine of transubstantiation. "Religion without it," he wrote, "is somber and illogical." Having recognized the power of words at the consecration of the Eucharist – words which, Catholics believe, transform ordinary bread and ordinary wine into the real body and real blood – never again could language prove merely decorative. For him, a consecration made from human language reversed existential randomness and estrangement, the experience of which shadowed many of his contemporaries. Assuming that human language possessed this power, Hopkins went on to untie the bindings and stretch the known limits of poetry. He obliged his few readers to expand their receptivity.

During the later 1870s, Hopkins's new voice would ring out in the nature sonnets: "God's Grandeur," "The Starlight Night," "Spring," "In the Valley of the Elwy," "The Sea and the Skylark,"

"The Windhover," "Pied Beauty," "Hurrahing in Harvest," "The Caged Skylark," "The Lantern out of Doors." One could say that Hopkins practiced transubstantiation in every poem. By mysterious talent, he changed plain element into reality sublime. He encountered a jumble of weather, birds, trees, branches, waters, blooms, dewdrops, candle flames, prayers, then instressed them and, delighted, wrote in his journal, "Chance left free to act falls into an order."

Transubstantiation also, for Hopkins, reorganized molecular disorder: instead of losing heat, as the laws of thermodynamics indicate, Creation rebooted every time divine power zapped the altar with the sacred words *hoc est corpus meum* (this is my body). The localization of power into, onto, everyday elements like bread and wine added to Hopkins's overall sense of compression, of the felt pressure, of the stressing inward, of religious meaning. And just as the determined and talented young boy Gerard had once forced his little brothers to eat flowers so that they would really understand flowers, the adult Gerard believed that only by eating the Eucharist could he "take in" (his word was "instress") God. The Incarnation of Christ raised the energy of everything. And when Hopkins placed his conviction of this into poetry, he tended to mention electricity, lightning, fire, flash, flame. He wrote in his late, great poem, "That Nature is a Heraclitean Fire and the comfort of the Resurrection": "In a flash, at a trumpet crash, / I am all at once what Christ is, | since he was what I am and / This jack, joke, poor potsherd, | patch matchwood, immortal diamond, / Is immortal diamond."

His posthumously collected poems were published in 1918, the final year of the World War which left western civilization gassed and devastated. All art would undergo transformation. Ironically, almost thirty years after his death, Hopkins's slight volume encapsulated like an unexploded bomb the energetic proof that he had already transformed English poetry. Today, more than a century and a quarter after his death, he is universally recognized among the greatest English poets. And his greatest greatness, I think, lies in his appropriation of nature to establish religious meaning. Nature, as he idiosyncratically saw it, fastened him to God. He "instressed" an "inscape" (pattern), and this act energized him and whatever he looked upon. And though he would spend the final five years of his life plagued by "fits of sadness so severe they resemble madness," Hopkins never abandoned the solution he had achieved through his reading of nature's explosive titration with God.

The mid-Victorian period, with its legacy of Romantic poetry and painting, produced many amateur naturalists. Observers repeatedly described Hopkins as stooping down to study wet sand or blades of grass or little blue flowers. When he was eighteen, he drew an excellent likeness of weeds which he labeled neatly, "Dandelion, Hemlock & Ivy." It was not unusual for nineteenth-century poets to associate nature with heightened emotional states, or even to bind it to the notion that God himself may have written nature like a book. This book could reveal the divine to those who had eyes to read. Keats had coined the phrase "egotistical sublime" to describe Wordsworth's enhanced self-consciousness in the presence of nature. Hopkins, on the other hand, instressed the sublime to enhance his other-consciousness.

Hopkins grew up in Wordsworth's and Keats's poetic shadows, in a household filled with good artists, and in an era that encouraged the close study of natural phenomena. He was raised to fulfill the expectations of a milieu that privileged certain pursuits of noble leisure – drawing, poetry, piety. Hopkins was gifted at all of these pursuits. His siblings were also talented, and in their lifetimes more obviously accomplished than he: Lionel became an internationally renowned scholar of ancient Chinese; Arthur illustrated Thomas Hardy; Millicent, an excellent musician, became an Anglican nun. His mother loved Dickens and German philosophy. She was a descendent of the painter Gainsborough. His father, an insurance executive, published religious poetry. Everything about his family made it probable that Hopkins would pursue a path marked by art and an Oxford identity. Improbable, however, was his conversion at twenty-two to Roman Catholicism, the and of a few rejected Oxford patricians like John Henry Newman and the younger Thomas Arnold.

The reactions of Hopkins's parents and friends to his conversion were predictably negative. The poet's father, Manley Hopkins, wrote to Canon Liddon:

> Save him from throwing a pure life and a somewhat unusual intellect away in the cold limbo which Rome assigns her English converts. The deepness of our distress, the shattering of our hopes & the foreseen estrangement which must happen, are my excuse for writing to you so freely & so pressingly; but even these motives do not weigh with us in comparison of our pity for our dear son.[5]

This sentiment persisted among Hopkins's associates for the rest of his life. A year after Hopkins died, Charles Luxmoore wrote to Arthur Hopkins: "Humanly speaking he made a grievous mistake in joining the Jesuits."

There were other Catholic converts, of course, including five undergraduates in Hopkins's class at Oxford. And there were other nature lovers, and other poets, like the Rossettis, drawn to a purer pre-Reformation past. But Hopkins eventually short-circuited all trends with his intrusive genius. You could say that he unintentionally spearheaded modernity in poetry. His closest friend, Bridges, buried Hopkins's work for thirty years, and then presented it to a readership not quite ready; only after the second edition of the *Poems* came out in 1930, after Modernism and Imagism and free verse, did Hopkins's confounding and game-changing contribution take off. It strutted the unabashed two-beat foot of common speech ("rash smart sloggering brine") and Anglo-Saxonate kennings (wanwood, betweenpie, leafmeal). His new style reached all the way back, and all the way forward.

Hopkins's legacy contains nagging contradictions: a master religious poet in the category of Donne and Herbert, he abandoned tradition by architecting wild verbal experiments. And then, he constantly protested his indifference to critical opinion and thus to poetic fame: he wrote to Robert Bridges, "You are my audience and I plan to convert you." When accused of outwriting the wits of even this audience, he refused to give an inch: "I cannot think of altering anything. Why shd. I?" It seems, though, that while perhaps indifferent to fame, he certainly intended to broadcast something he kept seeing – that constant, recurrent presence of God. What indeed could anybody say?

By the end of his life, though he did not know he would soon die of typhoid (caused by antiquated plumbing in the Jesuit residence at 86 Stephen's Green, Dublin), Hopkins complained in aggrieved sonnets, "Soul self, come poor Jackself, I do advise / You, jaded, let be" and "Birds build, but not I build; no, but strain / Time's eunuch and not breed one work that wakes." He felt far-flung, flattened, a failure. He was not destined to live long enough to reverse this feeling. If only he could have known that eventually Christians and literary critics alike would be ecstatic to claim him as their own: "Somewhat to their surprise . . . the public are being told by the best critics . . . that an English Jesuit who died over forty years ago must be regarded as one of England's greatest poets."[6] Ultimately readers would find in Hopkins's words a refreshing, liberating way of receiving and holding the body of God.

IN THE NEXT SECTION of this volume, "Christ Calls," some of Hopkins's early written material – poems, journal entries, and letters – will point the way to his later achievement. The poems express delirious idealism about religious life ("Heaven-Haven"), an early reflection on the sacramental possibilities of bread and wine ("Barnfloor and Winepress"), a sonnet written when he was twenty-one ("Myself Unholy"). His perceived unholiness also appears in scrupulously kept confessional notes, which include lists of sins such as oversleeping, talking too much, and looking at anatomical drawings in *The Lancet*. His scrupulosity was extreme, and it seems certain that Hopkins was a controlled, lifelong celibate.

The self-restraint he exerted from the time he decided on a religious vocation (1868) meant that he wrote no poetry for seven years; that same self-restraint created an ambitious, tempestuous, dramatic, iconoclastic, debut masterpiece in "The Wreck of the Deutschland" (1875–76), which he actually wrote under obedience. We will read this poem in Part III, "Reckoning with the Wreck."

In 1872, three years before he determined that he was permitted to write poetry, Hopkins discovered the medieval Franciscan Duns Scotus's commentary on Lombard's *Sentences* (1250). Although his appropriation of Scotus (1266–1308) alienated his Jesuit examiners in the theologate (who preferred the teachings of the "Angelic Doctor," Thomas Aquinas), Hopkins acquired both inspiration and consolation from Scotus's special take on the well-worn medieval dialectic concerning universals and particulars. Hopkins's sonnet "Duns Scotus' Oxford" claims that the Franciscan "of all men most sways my spirit to peace." For Scotus, individual things always resulted from a process he called "contraction," by which universals contracted down into *haecceitas,* the "thisness" of particular concrete things. So affirmed by Scotus, Hopkins will write "Each mortal thing does one thing and the same: / Selves – goes itself; myself it speaks and spells, / Crying What I do is me: for that I came." Here Hopkins reveals what I consider his most significant contribution to the arts of living morally and of writing uniquely: the concept of "selving." He cobbles it from an arcane point in Scotus's commentary, runs with it, and from it springs the real originality of Hopkins's opus. His idea of selving blends with a Victorian taste for precise detail. I believe that his discovery of Scotus enabled him to write the poems of the late 1870s, and determined how he would write them. We will read his nature poems in Part IV, "What I Do Is Me."

The final section, "Wrestling with God," will include writing from the last five years of his life (1884–89). Happiest as an undergraduate at "Cuckoo-echoing, bell-swarmèd, lark-charmèd, rook-racked" Oxford (1864–67), and then again during the theologate at St. Beuno's "on a pastoral forehead" in Wales (1874–77), Hopkins proved ill-suited to working long, humble hours as a priest and academic examiner in the industrial slums to which his vocation sent him. Liverpool, Chesterfield, London, Glasgow, finally Dublin: the absence of larks and cuckoos compounded by his own apparent lack of talent in transacting his priestly assignments drained him. For most of his clerical career, he complained of extreme exhaustion and its handmaiden, depression. He described himself as "harried" and "fagged" and "gallied up and down." None of us likes to do what we are not good at doing. Hopkins's claim that his religious vocation "selved" him must have been often challenged. Still, even in despondency, he never quit but rather conducted an extremely robust if solitary conversation with the universe.

PART II

Benenden, Kent,
fr. Hemsted Park.
Oct. 11. 1863

Christ Calls

HERE IS THE GENERAL NARRATIVE of Hopkins's religious conversion: born in England in 1844 into high culture and wealth, he would have been expected to pursue noble leisure and to worship as a conventional Anglican. That he was oppositional to authority as a schoolboy (sassing his headmaster) and strange as a child (forcing his little brothers to eat flowers) foretold a personality prone to real originality. His early practice of intense self-examination, of carefully recording in his commonplace book his slightest sins, prophesied his later moral scrupulosity. Leslie Higgins, general editor of the new *Collected Works of Gerard Manley Hopkins*, writes:

> Hopkins was 20 and 21 during that "self-wrung, selfstrung" year between Lent 1865 and Lent 1866, yet many of the "sins" seem strikingly adolescent: looking up provocative words in the dictionary; noting keenly the bodies of other people; fixating on genitalia (in a statue, a painting, a dog); mooning over one's first major unrequited crush. . . .
>
> Initially, the lists of transgressions occupy two or three lines of the small diary. Within months, however, the near and actual occasion for "sins" is consuming both the page and the young man's life. (As he later observed of his friend Geldart, Hopkins was "a selftormentor.") Few aspects of daily existence were not jeopardizing, whether dining with friends, eating biscuits, staying in bed

too long in the mornings, not going to bed early enough at night, gossiping, mocking his father's mannerisms, being impatient with siblings. He also frequently chastised himself for "forecasting" a desire to convert (especially in autumn 1865). Ever the extremist, Hopkins seized the momentum of self-loathing all too avidly – a pattern that would be repeated throughout the next two and a half decades.[7]

Yet even with ample evidence of his unpredictability, his conversion to Roman Catholicism proved an unpleasant surprise to his friends and relatives.

First, some background on the entrenched phenomenon of anti-Catholicism in Victorian England: from the time of the ambiguously-named English Reformation, the public status of identifying as a Roman Catholic ranged from tolerance (during the reign of Mary Tudor, for example, 1553–58) to a sentence of high treason (during the reign of Elizabeth I, 1558–1604), punishable by public death by hideous torture. As decades passed, England loosened its religious prohibitions, but the Anglican Church, with its Thirty-Nine Articles and *Book of Common Prayer*, dominated the land and even the empire. There was no separation of church from state. As recently as the early twentieth century, Roman Catholics were viewed as undesirable outsiders. And for many decades after the Elizabethan Settlement of 1559 (which banished the pope and the doctrine of transubstantiation, among other basic Roman Catholic markers), Catholics had to hide as recusants, attend Mass in secret, stash their priests in closets, forego owning property, and abstain from travel beyond five miles from the place of their birth.

In seventeenth-century Ireland, Catholic priests were hunted down with horses and hounds and murdered. In England as well, Catholics were regarded as threats to the security of the

Protestant nation, and the pope was considered a foreign enemy. After the passing of centuries without episodes of Catholic aggression, however, Parliament gradually relaxed, culminating in the Act of Catholic Emancipation in 1829. When Rome re-established a Cardinal, Henry Manning, at Westminster, London in 1850, though, crowds protested. There were anti-Catholic riots and burnings in effigy of Catholic bishops that recalled the Guy Fawkes affair of 1605 (remembered in England to this day every November 5). Of the forty thousand novels published under the long reign of Queen Victoria, many thousands included anti-Catholic themes.

In the year of the Great Reform Bill, 1832, a religious trend began at Oxford University, called the Oxford Movement (or the Tractarian Movement, because its participants published tracts). Members of both Senior and Junior Common Rooms joined in seeking to redeem the boredom and tepid flaccidity of Anglicanism by reintroducing some of the more interesting doctrines of the pre-Reformation past. Though initially identified with tracts on ecclesiastical subjects, the movement eventually included the rise of Gothic architecture and with it, medieval-style ceremony, the use of vestments, the practice of auricular confession, and the opening of Anglican religious orders. Historians generally mark the official "end" of the Oxford Movement at 1845 when its most famous leader – the former chaplain to Oxford University, John Henry Newman – went over to Rome, ultimately bringing a posse of Tractarians with him. After Newman's departure from the university, however, the group was called "Puseyites," after Dr. Edward Pusey, Regius Professor of Hebrew. When Gerard Manley Hopkins arrived at Oxford in 1864, he attended Sunday evenings with Canon Henry Liddon, a strong follower of Pusey and Tractarianism.

Had Hopkins stopped there, we would almost certainly not be reading about him right now. He would have spent Sundays with like-minded Anglicans, remained at Oxford, become a professor of Greek, and, presumably, sketched landscapes on his walking holidays. He might have gone on writing poems like "Heaven-Haven: A nun takes the veil." Instead, he took a "veil" himself – on January 23, 1866 he wrote his famous diary entry, "For Lent. No pudding on Sundays. . . . No verses in Passion Week or on Fridays." (So, in an ascetical resolution, he restricts his engagement with poetry.) On July 17, he noted in his journal "the impossibility of staying in the Church of England." On October 15, he wrote to John Henry Newman about his decision to convert; one day later, in a letter, he announced his conversion to his father. When his father inquired if he had considered that this would alienate him from his family, Hopkins replied in the affirmative. On the other hand, for every loss, there was apparently compensation: he wrote to William Urquhart that he knew "the first complete peace of mind I have ever had."

What happened next is legendary among those who know Hopkins's biography – he wrote to Urquhart saying "my conversion when it came was all in a minute" (Letter of October 4, 1866). He then left Oxford to teach in Newman's Oratory School in Birmingham. He strongly sensed an increasing conflict between his personal inclinations (poetry, for example) and his religious vocation. He burned his poems. In 1868, he joined the Jesuits. Like all new Jesuits, he undertook the demanding, life-changing Thirty-Day Retreat with *The Spiritual Exercises of St. Ignatius Loyola*. He completed two years of novitiate (1868–70), took vows of poverty, chastity, and obedience, and put on the Roman collar. He studied for his philosophate at Stonyhurst (1870–73). His life as a Catholic stirred his compassion for the poor. One letter written from Stonyhurst (April 1871) to Robert

Bridges has been called Hopkins's "red" letter. In it he refers to himself as a "Communist":

> But it is a dreadful thing for the greatest and most necessary part of a very rich nation to live a hard life without dignity, knowledge, comforts, delight, or hopes in the midst of plenty – which plenty they make.

During these years, he kept a journal filled with what he seemed not to have known was potential poetry. Many of the journal entries concerned the weather:

> *July 1 [1866].* Sharp showers, bright between. Late in the afternoon, the light and shade being brilliant, snowy blocks of cloud were filing over the sky and under the sun hanging above and along the earth-line were those multitudinous up-and-down crispy sparkling chains with pearly shadows up to the edges. At sunset, wh. was in a grey bank with moist gold dabs and racks, the whole round of skyline had level clouds naturally lead-colour but the upper parts ruddied, some more, some less rosy. Spits or gleams braided or built in with slanting pellet flakes made their way. Through such clouds anvil-shaped pink ones and up-blown fleece-of-wool flat-topped dangerous-looking pieces.

Hopkins's journals, like his letters, contain the same jolting, irregular phrases which will spring into the rhythm of his mature poetry.

In 1874 Hopkins moved to St. Beuno's College in Wales to pursue the theologate, and there he wrote "The Wreck of the Deutschland." His journal stopped. He then entered high gear as a poet who wrote ten major poems in less than one year, was ordained a priest (1877), left Wales, and did much apparently grueling parish work. In preparation for Final Vows, which Jesuits take thirteen years after First Vows, he made tertianship (1881–82) and another Thirty-Day Retreat, during which he experienced a nervous breakdown. After Final Vows, he moved to Dublin (1884) to teach at Newman's failing Catholic University, sank into a five-year depression, wrote the "terrible sonnets," wrote "That Nature is a Heraclitean Fire" (1888), and died of typhoid fever at the age of forty-four in 1889.

This terse chronology omits the early triumphs that rested on Gerard Manley Hopkins like a bright mantle until he became a Catholic; after that, usually, when he undertook priestly work, he seemed doomed to profound exhaustion. Another convert, Evelyn Waugh, explains that there was nothing pretty about English Catholicism:

> My readers outside England should understand that the aesthetic appeal of the Church of England is unique and peculiar in those islands. Elsewhere a first interest in the Catholic Church is often kindled in the convert's imagination by the splendors of her worship in contrast with the bleakness and meanness of the Protestant sects. In England the pull is all the other way. The medieval cathedrals and churches, the rich ceremonies that surround the monarchy, the historic titles of Canterbury and York, the social organization of the country parishes, the traditional culture of Oxford and Cambridge, the liturgy composed in the heyday of English prose style – all these are the property of the Church of England, while Catholics meet in modern buildings, often of deplorable design, and are usually served by simple Irish missionaries.[8]

Arguably Roman Catholicism taught Hopkins more than private drawing lessons, prep school, or Oxford could have about being a great deviser of major art. His celebration of the nature he observed approaches but skirts the pantheism of his Romantic predecessors. The way he saw beauty caused lines like this to break from him: "The heart rears wings . . . / and hurls for him, O half hurls earth for him off under his feet." His former schoolteacher Richard Watson Dixon, an Anglican clergyman, tried to console Hopkins into thinking of his verses "as a means of serving . . . religion." But Hopkins replied that writing poetry was "a waste of time." Surely no other major poet has ever thought of his own work as a waste of time.

In this fallen setting, Hopkins doubted himself. Never, however, did he seem to doubt his conversion. And the self-compression and self-restraint required by his vocation, the "holding of himself back," would become the best hammer and anvil for his genius. He became, in the judgment of others, isolated, melancholic, and idiosyncratic. Yet his letters were energetic, his journal entries vital and inventive, and his relatively few mature poems fantastically ambitious. The preeminent detail about both Hopkins and his extraordinary body of writing is surely that he foregrounded theological considerations. For him, a world without a living God would have been unthinkable.

When Hopkins was young and merely a highly strung Anglican, he felt strong loves and delights: to his mother he wrote from Oxford (1864), "Except for much work and that I can never keep my hands cool, I am almost too happy." He went to wine parties every day and was described as "popular with classmates." Although within two years he would leave Oxford and abandon the future he surely would have enjoyed there, he never lost his gentleman's loyalty to the place. In 1880, fourteen years after becoming a Catholic, he wrote to his Oxford friend Mowbray Baillie, "Not to love my university would be to undo the very buttons of my being."

And yet, for all this zest and apparent *joie de vivre* at the time of his conversion, when he entered the passage in his diary, resolving "No pudding on Sundays" and other little foreswearings, he demonstrated a personality apparently born with a predilection for difficulty. Indeed, his brand of quaint asceticism was popular among the post-Tractarians at Oxford. Dr. Pusey himself kept custody of the eyes. But as Hopkins made his pious resolutions, he also wrote in his diary, "Grey clouds in knops" and "Eyelids like leaves, petals, caps, tufted hats, handkerchiefs, sleeves, gloves" – like the verbal virtuoso he was unconsciously rehearsing to become.

E. H. Coleridge, grandson of the Romantic poet Samuel Taylor Coleridge, was a religiously inclined classmate of Hopkins at Balliol. The day before Hopkins recorded his Lenten resolution to eschew pudding and so on, he wrote to young Coleridge an important credo which illuminates not only his sense of being "called," but of being called to read the world through the lens of the Incarnation and of the sacramental view that constantly mirrors it: "I think that the trivialness of life is . . . done away with by the Incarnation. . . . Our Lord submitted not only to the pains of life, the fasting, scourging, crucifixion etc., or the insults, as the mocking, blindfolding, spitting etc., but also to the mean and trivial accidents of humanity."

Roman Catholicism in general, and the Jesuit order in particular, offered Hopkins elements that he craved constitutionally, and then provided him with the follow-through to become the self he was meant to be – an ingenious but hidden poet, a priest exhausted by his own scrupulosity, a "Jack, joke, poor potsherd" with bleeding hemorrhoids and failing eyesight, an "immortal diamond." He was destined to realize his purpose in the doctrines of incarnation, transubstantiation, and resurrection; in the radical ascesis of *The Spiritual Exercises of St. Ignatius Loyola;* and in the Mass itself.

When, as a boy, he made his little brothers eat flowers, this action proved predictive of his lifelong mind: he said he became a Roman Catholic mostly because the Sacrament of the Altar contained the real presence of Christ, and this he had to eat. He felt every step of the way a need to instress, to take in and gulp down, the proof of God's presence. Whether he could also express that proof as a ministry to others was uncertain. Before taking holy orders, at age twenty-four, he wrote to Baillie: "I want to write still and as a priest I very likely can do that too, not so freely as I shd. have liked, e.g., nothing or little in the verse way, but no doubt what would best serve the cause of my religion."

Eventually, he did produce great verse, and in all of it nature and theology blend like combustible chemicals producing a sparkling solution under the influence of high heat. His entire career, poetic and spiritual, launched a campaign against cliché and blur. He chose to suppress his instinct to write poetry to serve a "higher end," and yet he managed to produce great art.

At the foot of the
Reichenbach – July 18

Poems

(1864–1868)

Barnfloor and Winepress

"And he said, If the Lord do not help thee, whence shall I help thee?
out of the barnfloor, or out of the winepress?"

— *2 Kings 6:27*

Thou that on sin's wages starvest,
Behold we have the joy in Harvest:
For us was gathered the first-fruits
For us was lifted from the roots,
Sheaved in cruel bands, bruised sore,
Scourged upon the threshing-floor;
Where the upper mill-stone roof'd His Head,
At morn we found the Heavenly Bread,
    And on a thousand Altars laid,
      Christ our Sacrifice is made.

Those whose dry plot for moisture gapes,
We shout with them that tread the grapes:
For us the Vine was fenced with thorn,
Five ways the precious branches torn;
Terrible fruit was on the tree
In the Acre of Gethsemane;
For us by Calvary's distress
The wine was rackèd from the press;
    Now in our Altar vessels stored
      Is the sweet Vintage of our Lord.

In Joseph's garden they threw by
The riv'n Vine, leafless, lifeless, dry:
On Easter morn the Tree was forth,
In forty days reach'd Heaven from earth,
    Soon the whole world is overspread;
      Ye weary come into the shade.

The field where He has planted us
Shall shake his boughs as Libanus,
When He hath sheaved us in His sheaf,
When He has made us bear His leaf.
    We scarcely call that Banquet food,
    But even our Saviour's and our blood,
    We are so grafted on His Wood.

Myself unholy, from myself unholy

Myself unholy, from myself unholy
To the sweet living of my friends I look –
Eye-greeting doves bright-counter to the rook,
Fresh brooks to salt sand-teasing waters shoaly:
And they are purer, but alas not solely
The unquestion'd readings of a blotless book.
And so my trust, confused, struck, and shook
Yields to the sultry siege of melancholy.
He has a sin of mine, he its near brother,
Knowing them well I can but see the fall.
This fault in one I found, that in another:
And so, though each have one while I have all,
No *better* serves me now, save *best;* no other
Save Christ: to Christ I look, on Christ I call.

Let Me Be to Thee as the Circling Bird

Let me be to Thee as the circling bird,
Or bat with tender and air-crisping wings
That shapes in half-light his departing rings,
From both of whom a changeless note is heard.
I have found my music in a common word,
Trying each pleasurable throat that sings
And every praisèd sequence of sweet strings,
And know infallibly which I preferred.
The authentic cadence was discovered late

Which ends those only strains that I approve,
And other science all gone out of date
And minor sweetness scarce made mention of:
I have found the dominant of my range and state –
Love, O my God, to call thee Love and Love.

The Habit of Perfection

Elected Silence, sing to me
And beat upon my whorlèd ear,
Pipe me to pastures still and be
The music that I care to hear.

Shape nothing, lips; be lovely-dumb:
It is the shut, the curfew sent
From there where all surrenders come
Which only makes you eloquent.

Be shellèd, eyes, with double dark
And find the uncreated light:
This ruck and reel which you remark
Coils, keeps, and teases simple sight.

Palate, the hutch of tasty lust,
Desire not to be rinsed with wine:
The can must be so sweet, the crust
So fresh that come in fasts divine!

Nostrils, your careless breath that spend
Upon the stir and keep of pride,
What relish shall the censers send
Along the sanctuary side!

O feel-of-primrose hands, O feet
That want the yield of plushy sward,
But you shall walk the golden street
And you unhouse and house the Lord.

And, Poverty, be thou the bride
And now the marriage feast begun,
And lily-coloured clothes provide
Your spouse not laboured-at nor spun.

Heaven–Haven

A nun takes the veil

I have desired to go
    Where springs not fail,
To fields where flies no sharp and sided hail
    And a few lilies blow.

And I have asked to be
    Where no storms come,
Where the green swell is in the havens dumb,
    And out of the swing of the sea.

Letters

(1866–1874)

To E. H. Coleridge, January 22, 1866, from Oxford

Coleridge was the grandson of Samuel Taylor Coleridge, and a schoolboy friend of Hopkins.

Dear Coleridge . . . it is incredible and intolerable if there is nothing which is the reverse of trivial and will correct and avenge the triviality of this life. To myself all this trivialness is one of the strongest reasons for the opposite belief and is always in action more or less. Of course it is plain too that the belief in the future of theology destroys the triviality in proportion to its intensity. . . . I think that the trivialness of life is, and personally to each one, ought to be seen to be, done away with by the Incarnation – or, I shd. say the difficulty wh. the trivialness of life presents ought to be. It is one adorable point of the incredible condescension of the Incarnation (the greatness of which no saint can have ever hoped to realise) that our Lord submitted not only to the pains of life, the fasting, scourging, crucifixion etc., or the insults, as the mocking, blindfolding, spitting etc., but also to the mean and trivial accidents of humanity. It leads one naturally to rhetorical antithesis to think for instance that after making the world He shd. consent to be taught carpentering, and, being the eternal Reason, to be catechised in the theology of the Rabbins. It seems therefore that if the Incarnation cd. [take place among] trivial men and trivial things it is not surprising that our reception or non-reception of its benefits shd. be also amidst trivialities.

Gerard Hopkins

Robert Bridges became Hopkins's close friend while at Oxford, and remained so throughout his life. Despite Bridges's antipathy to Roman Catholicism, he among all of Hopkins's friends took best care of his poems, often retaining the only copy. Bridges was a medical doctor; he also maintained an active literary life, about which he corresponded with Hopkins. Eventually Bridges became poet laureate of England (1913–30). He introduced and posthumously published the first edition of Hopkins's poems in 1918.

To Robert Bridges, September 24, 1866, from Hampstead

Dear Bridges . . . Dr. Newman was most kind, I mean in the very best sense, for his manner is not that of solicitous kindness but genial and almost, so to speak, unserious. And if I may say so, he was so sensible. He asked questions which made it clear for me how to act; I will tell you presently what that is: he made sure I was acting deliberately and wished to hear my arguments; when I had given them and said I cd. see no way out of them, he laughed and said 'Nor can I': and he told me I must come to the church to accept and believe – as I hope I do. He thought there appeared no reason, if it had not been for matters at home of course, why I shd. not be received at once, but in no way did he urge me on, rather the other way. . . .

You were surprised and sorry, you said, and possibly hurt that I wd. not tell you of my conversion till my going to Birmingham made it impossible any longer to conceal it. I was never sorry for one minute: it wd. have been culpably dishonourable and ungrateful, as I said before, not to have done one's best to conceal it: but I do not mean that, but this – the happiness it has been the means of bringing me I cd. not have conceived: I can never thank you enough for yr. kindness at that time. Notwithstanding my anxiety, which on the day we filled the aquarium was very great indeed, it gives me more delight to think of the time at Rochdale than any other time whatever that I can remember. . . .

Believe me, dear Bridges, with the utmost gratitude your very affectionate friend,

Gerard Hopkins

To John Henry Newman, October 15, 1866

Very Reverend Father, – I have been up at Oxford just long enough to have heard fr. my father and mother in return for my letter announcing my conversion. Their answers are terrible: I cannot read them twice. If you will pray for them and me just now I shall be deeply thankful. But what I am writing for is this – they urge me with the utmost entreaties to wait till I have taken my degree – more than half a year. Of course it is impossible, and since it is impossible to wait as long as they wish, it seems to me useless to wait at all. Wd. you therefore wish me to come to Birmingham at once, on Thursday, Friday, or Saturday? You will understand why I have any hesitation at all, namely because if immediately after their letters urging a long delay I am received without any, it will be another blow and look like intentional cruelty. I did not know till last night the rule about *communicatio in sacris* – at least as binding catechumens, but I now see the alternative thrown open, either to live without Church and sacraments or else, in order to avoid the Catholic Church, to have to attend constantly the services of that very Church. This brings the matter to an absurdity and makes me think that any delay, whatever relief it may be to my parents, is impossible. I am asking you then whether I shall at all costs be received at once. . . .

Believe me, dear Father, your affectionate son in Christ,

Gerard M. Hopkins

To his father, October 16, 1866, from Oxford

Dear Father, – I must begin with a practical immediate point. The Church strictly forbids all communion in sacred things with non-Catholics. I have only just learnt this, but it prevents me going to chapel, and so yesterday I had to inform the Dean of Chapel. Today the Master sent for me and said he cd. not grant me leave of absence without an application from you. As the College last term passed a resolution admitting Catholics and took a Catholic into residence it has no right to alter its principle in my case. I wish you therefore not to give yourself the pain of making this application, even if you were willing: I am of age moreover and am alone concerned. If you refuse to make the application, the Master explains that he shall lay my case before the common-room. In this case there is very little doubt indeed that the Fellows wd. take the reasonable course and give me leave of absence fr. chapel, and if not, I am quite contented: but in fact I am satisfied as to the course our Fellows will take and the Master will at the last hesitate to lay the matter before them perhaps even. I want you therefore to write at once, if you will, – not to the Master who has no right to ask what he does, but to me, with a refusal: no harm will follow.

The following is the position of things with me. You ask me to suspend my judgment for a long time, or at the very least more than half a year, in other words to stand still for a time. Now to stand still is not possible, thus: I must either obey the Church or disobey. If l disobey, I am not suspending judgment but deciding, namely, to take backward steps fr. the grounds I have already come to. To stand still if it were possible might be justifiable, but to go back nothing can justify. I must therefore obey the Church by ceasing to attend any service of the Church of England. If I am to wait then I must either be altogether without services and sacraments, which you will of course know is impossible, or else I must attend the services of the Church – still being unreceived. But what can be more contradictory than, in order to avoid joining the Church, attending the services of that very Church? Three of my friends, whose conversions were later than mine, Garrett, Addis, and Wood, have already been received, but this is by the way. Only one thing remains to be done: I cannot fight against God Who calls me to His Church: if I were to delay and die in the meantime I shd. have no plea why my soul was not forfeit. I have no power in fact to stir a finger: it is God Who makes the decision and not I.

But you do not understand what is involved in asking me to delay and how little good you wd. get from it. I shall hold as a Catholic what I have long held as an Anglican, that literal truth of our Lord's words by which I learn that the least fragment of the consecrated elements in the Blessed Sacrament of the Altar is the whole Body of Christ born of the Blessed Virgin, before which the whole host of saints and angels as it lies on the altar trembles with adoration. This belief once got is the life of the soul and when I doubted it I shd. become an atheist the next day. But, as Monsignor Eyre says, it is a gross superstition unless guaranteed by infallibility. I cannot hold this doctrine confessedly except as a Tractarian or a Catholic: the Tractarian ground I have seen broken to pieces under my feet. What end then can be served by a delay in wh. I shd. go on believing this doctrine as long as I believed in God and shd. be by the fact of my belief drawn by a lasting strain towards the Catholic Church?

About my hastiness I wish to say this. If the question, "which is the Church of Christ?" cd. only be settled by laborious search, a year and ten years and a lifetime are too little, when the vastness of the subject of theology is taken into account. But God must have made his Church such as to attract and convince the poor and unlearned as well as the learned. And surely it is true, though it will sound pride to say it, that the judgment of one who has seen both sides for a week is better than his who has seen only one for a lifetime. I am surprised you shd. say fancy and aesthetic tastes have led me to my present state of mind: these wd. be better satisfied in the Church of England, for bad taste is always meeting one in the accessories of Catholicism. My conversion is due to the following reasons mainly (I have put them down without order) (i) simple and strictly drawn arguments partly my own, partly others', (ii) common sense, (iii) reading the Bible, especially the Holy Gospels, where texts like 'Thou art Peter' (the evasions proposed for this alone are enough to make one a Catholic) and the manifest position of St. Peter among the Apostles so pursued me that at one time I thought it best to stop thinking of them, (iv) an increasing knowledge of the Catholic system (at first under the form of Tractarianism, later in its genuine place), which only wants to be known in order to be loved – its consolations, its marvelous ideal of holiness, the faith and devotion of its children, its multiplicity, its array of saints and martyrs, its consistency and unity, its glowing prayers, the daring majesty of its claims, etc. etc. You speak of the claims of the Church of England, but it is to me the strange thing that the Church of England makes no claims: it is true that Tractarians make them for her and find them faintly or only in a few instances borne out for them by her liturgy, and are strongly assailed for their extravagances while they do it. Then about applying to Mr. Liddon and the Bp. of Oxford. Mr. Liddon writes begging me to pause: it wd. take too long to explain how I did not apply to him at first and why it wd. have been useless. If Dr. Pusey is in Oxford tomorrow I will see him, if it is any satisfaction to you. The Bishop is too much engaged to listen to individual difficulties and those who do apply to him may get such answers as young Mr. Lane Fox did, who gave up £30,000 a year just lately to become a Catholic. He wrote back about a cob which he wanted to sell to the Dean of some place and wh. Lane Fox was to put his own price on and ride over for the Bishop to the place of sale. In fact Dr. Pusey and Mr. Liddon were the only two men in the world who cd. avail to detain me: the fact that they were Anglicans kept me one, for arguments for the Church of England I had long ago felt there were none that wd. hold water, and when that influence gave way everything was gone.

You are so kind as not to forbid me your house, to which I have no claim, on condition, if I understand, that I promise not to try to convert my brothers and sisters. Before I can promise this I must get permission, wh. I have no doubt will be given. Of course this promise will not apply after they come of age. Whether after my reception you will still speak as you do now I cannot tell.

You ask me if I have had no thought of the estrangement. I have had months to think of everything. Our Lord's last care on the cross was to commend His mother to His Church and His Church to His mother in the person of St. John. If even now you wd. put yourselves into that position wh. Christ so unmistakeably gives us and ask the Mother of sorrows to remember her three hours' compassion at the cross, the piercing of the sword prophesied by Simeon, and her seven dolours, and her spouse Joseph, the lily of chastity, to remember the flight into Egypt, the searching for his Foster-Son at twelve years old, and his last ecstasy with Christ at his death-bed, the prayers of this Holy Family wd. in a few days put an end to estrangements forever. If you shrink fr. doing this, though the Gospels cry aloud to you to do it, at least for once – if you like, only once – approach Christ in a new way in which you will at all events feel that you are exactly in unison with me, that is, not vaguely, but casting yourselves into His sacred broken Heart and His five adorable Wounds. Those who do not pray to Him in His Passion pray to God but scarcely to Christ. I have the right to propose this, for I have tried both ways, and if you will not give one trial to this way you will see you are prolonging the estrangement and not I.

After saying this I feel lighter-hearted, though I still can by no means make my pen write what I shd. wish. I am your loving son.

Gerard M. Hopkins

P.S. I am most anxious that you shd. not think of my future. It is likely that the positions you wd. like to see me in wd. have no attraction for me, and surely the happiness of my prospects depends on the happiness to me and not on intrinsic advantages. It is possible even to be very sad and very happy at once and the time that I was with Bridges, when my anxiety came to its height, was I believe, the happiest fortnight of my life. My only strong wish is to be independent.

If you are really willing to make the application to the Master, well and good; but I do not want you to put yourself to pain. I have written a remonstrance to him.

Many thanks to Arthur for his letter.

Hopkins's parents quite quickly resumed contact with him after he became a Catholic. A semester later, Hopkins left Oxford to teach at Newman's Oratory School. From there he wrote the following letter to Alexander William Mowbray Baillie, the son of an Edinburgh doctor. He and Hopkins had both qualified for a Balliol "Domus" scholarship from Oxford. Baillie's rational mind was said to have been "a very valuable quality in him for those of his friends who possessed the artistic temperament."9

To A. W. M. Baillie, February 12, 1868, from Edgbaston

My dear Baillie, . . . I must say that I am very anxious to get away from this place. I have become very weak in health and do not seem to recover myself here or likely to do so. Teaching is very burdensome, especially when you have much of it: I have. I have not much time and almost no energy – for I am always tired – to do anything on my own account. I put aside that one sees and hears nothing and nobody here. Very happily Challis of Merton is now here; else the place were without reservation 'damned, shepherd'. (This is not swearing.) I ought to make the exception that the boys are very nice indeed. I am expecting to take orders and soon, but I wish it to be secret till it comes about. Besides that it is the happiest and best way it practically is the only one.

You know I once wanted to be a painter. But even if I could I wd. not I think, now, for the fact is that the higher and more attractive parts of the art put a strain upon the passions which I shd. think it unsafe to encounter. I want to write still and as a priest I very likely can do that too, not so freely as I shd. have liked, e.g. nothing or little in the verse way, but no doubt what wd. best serve the cause of my religion. But if I am a priest it will cause my mother, or she says it will, great grief and this preys on my mind very much and makes the near prospect quite black. The general result is that I am perfectly reckless about things that I shd. otherwise care about, uncertain as I am whether in a few months I may not be shut up in a cloister, and this state of mind, though it is painful coming to, when reached gives a great and real sense of freedom. Do you happen to know of any tutorship I cd. take for a few months after Easter? as I am anxious to leave this place then and also not to leave it without having secured something to live upon till, as seems likely, I take minor orders. . . .

Believe me always your affectionate friend,

Gerard M. Hopkins

To Robert Bridges, August 2, 1871, from Stonyhurst

My dear Bridges, . . . I am afraid some great revolution is not far off. Horrible to say, in a manner I am a Communist. Their ideal bating some things is nobler than that professed by any secular statesman I know of (I must own I live in bat-light and shoot at a venture). Besides it is just. – I do not mean the means of getting to it are. But it is a dreadful thing for the greatest and most necessary part of a very rich nation to live a hard life without dignity, knowledge, comforts, delight, or hopes in the midst of plenty – which plenty they make. They profess that they do not care what they wreck and burn, the old civilisation and order must be destroyed. This is a dreadful look out but what has the old civilisation done for them? As it at present stands in England it is itself in great measure founded on wrecking. But they got none of the spoils, they came in for nothing but harm from it then and thereafter. England has grown hugely wealthy but this wealth has not reached the working classes; I expect it has made their condition worse. Besides this iniquitous order the old civilisation embodies another order mostly old and what is new in direct entail from the old, the old religion, learning, law, art, etc. and all the history that is preserved in standing monuments. But as the working classes have not been educated they know next to nothing of all this and cannot be expected to care if they destroy it. The more I look the more black and deservedly black the future looks, so I will write no more . . .

Believe me your affectionate friend,

Gerard Hopkins S.J.

Journals

(1864–1875)

Hopkins included relatively few personal notes in his journals, and those few reveal the quality of his own highly "stressed" character. Since he had forbidden himself his natural outlet of poetry, the journals became an outpouring of self-expression. Higgins describes them as "the counterpoint to days of study, whether academic or theological. There are times, however, when he slips back into the self-reporting mode, feeling emotionally bruised. Hopkins is, first and last, a textual being. . . ."[10] The entries oscillate between ecstatic descriptions of natural phenomena and painful self-examination. After 1875, when he ceased keeping journals, the stress and compression that marked his nature took both form and content in his verse once again.

1864

January 27. Two swans flew high up over the river on which I was, their necks stretched straight out and wings billowing.

Note on green wheat. The difference between this green and that of long grass is that first suggests silver, latter azure. Former more opacity, body, smoothness. It is the exact complement of carnation.

Nearest to emerald of any green I know, the real emerald *stone*. It is lucent. Perhaps it has a chrysoprase [golden-green stone] bloom. Both blue greens.

It is a happy thing that there is no royal road to poetry. The world shd. know by this time that one cannot reach Parnassus except by flying thither. Yet fr. time to time more men go up and either perish in its gullies fluttering *excelsior* flags or else come down again with full folios and blank countenances. Yet the old fallacy keeps its ground. Every age has its false alarms.

The poetical language lowest. To use that, wh. poetasters, and indeed almost everyone, can do, is no more necessarily to be uttering poetry than striking the keys of piano is playing a tune. Only, when the tune is played it is on the keys. So when poetry is uttered it is in this language. Next, Parnassian. Can only be used by real poets. Can be written without inspiration. Good instance in *Enoch Arden's* island.[11] Common in professedly descriptive pieces. Much of it in *Paradise Lost* and *Regained*. Nearly all *The Faery Queen*. It is the effect of fine age to enable ordinary people to write something very near it. – Third and highest poetry proper, language of inspiration. Explain inspiration. On first reading a strange poet his merest Parnassian seems inspired. This is because then first we perceive genius. But when we have read more of him and are accustomed to the genius we shall see distinctly the inspirations and much that wd. have struck us with great pleasure at first loses much of its charm and becomes Parnassian. – Castalian, highest sort of Parnassian. e.g. "Yet despair touches me not, Tho' pensive as a bird Whose vernal coverts winter hath laid bare."[12] . . . Much Parnassian takes down a poet's reputation, lowers his average, as it were. Pope and all artificial schools great writers of Parnassian. This is the real meaning of an artificial poet.

May 3. Cold. Morning raw and wet, afternoon fine. Walked then with Addis, crossing Bablock Hythe, round by Skinner's Weir through many fields into the Witney road. Sky sleepy blue without liquidity. Fr. Cumnor Hill saw St. Philip's and the other spires through blue haze rising pale in a pink light. On further side of the Witney road hills, just fleeced with grain or other green growth, by their dips and waves foreshortened here and there and so differenced in brightness and opacity the green on them, with delicate effect. On left, brow of the near hill glistening with very bright newly turned sods and a scarf of vivid green slanting away beyond the skyline, against which the clouds shewed the slightest tinge of rose or purple. Copses in grey-red or greyyellow – the tinges immediately forerunning the opening of full leaf. Meadows skirting Seven-bridge road voluptuous green. Some oaks are out in small leaf. Ashes not out, only tufted with their fringy blooms. Hedges springing richly. Elms in small leaf, with more or less opacity. White poplars most beautiful in small grey crisp spray-like leaf. Cowslips capriciously colouring meadows in creamy drifts. Bluebells, purple orchis. Over the green water of the river passing the slums of the town and under its bridges swallows shooting, blue and purple above and shewing their amber-tinged breasts reflected in the water, their flight unsteady with wagging wings and leaning first to one side then the other. Peewits flying. Towards sunset the sky partly swept, as often, with moist white cloud, tailing off across which are morsels of grey-black woolly clouds. Sun seemed to make a bright liquid hole in this, its texture had an upward northerly sweep or drift fr. the West marked softly in grey. Dog violets. Eastward after sunset range of clouds rising in bulky heads moulded softly in tufts or bunches of snow – so it looks – and membered somewhat elaborately, rose-coloured. Notice often imperfect fairy rings. Apple and other fruit trees blossomed beautifully. . . .

June 30. Thunderstorms all day, great claps and lightning running up and down. When it was bright between times great towering clouds behind which the sun put out his shaded horns very clearly and a longish way. Level curds and whey sky after sunset. – Graceful growth of Etzkoltzias or however those unhappy flowers are spelt. Yews and evergreen trees now very thin and putting out their young pale shoots.

July 17. . . . It was this night I believe but possibly the next that I saw clearly the impossibility of staying in the Church of England, but resolved to say nothing to anyone till three months are over, that is the end of the Long, and then of course to take no step till after my Degree.

July 19. . . . Alone in the woods . . . I have now found the law of the oak leaves. . . .

"Found the law of the oak leaves"? At the heart of Hopkins's lifelong and consistent poetic reside the concepts of inscape and instress, thus named by Hopkins when he was an undergraduate. By "inscape" Hopkins means pattern in nature, and by "nature" he means not only oak leaves in the woods and clouds in the summer, but the more general reality of the universe, of "the way things are." For Hopkins, inscape results from divinely intelligent creation. Catherine Phillips, one editor of Hopkins's collected works, explains his idea of instress this way: "Unlike 'inscape,' which is the result of mental analysis and perception, 'instress' is more nebulous, often, although not always, associated with feeling; it is the identifying impression a thing can communicate to a careful and receptive observer. Hopkins also uses the term to mean 'the stress within,' the force which binds something or a person into a unit."[13] Those of us who have the eyes to see and the will to know can instress an inscape by not just "taking" it in, but by "stressing"

it in. "The law of the oak leaves" is their inscape; Hopkins "found"
that law on July 19, 1866, and instressed it.

1868

May 2. Fine, with some haze, and warm. This day, I think, I resolved.

May 5. Cold. Resolved to be a religious.

May 6. Fine but rather thick and with a very cold N.E. wind.

May 7. Warm; misty morning; then beautiful turquoise sky. Home,
after having decided to be a priest and religious but still doubtful
between St. Benedict and St. Ignatius. . . .

May 11. Dull; afternoon fine. Slaughter of the innocents. See above,
the 2nd.

July 11. . . . How fond of and warped to the mountains it wd. be easy
to become! For every cliff and limb and edge and jutty has its own
nobility. – Two boys came down the mountain yodeling. [Hopkins
is visiting Switzerland.] – We saw the snow in the hollows for the
first time. In one the surface was crisped across the direction of
the cleft and the other way, that is across the broader crisping and
down the stream, combed: the stream ran below and smoke came fr.
the hollow: the edge of the snow hewn in curves as if by moulding
planes. – Crowd of mountain flowers – gentians; gentianellas; blood-
red lucerne; a deep blue glossy spiked flower like plantain, flowering
gradually up the spike, so that at the top it looks like clover or
honeysuckle; rich big harebells glistening black like the cases of our
veins when dry and heated fr. without; and others. All the herbage
enthronged with every fingered or fretted leaf. – Firs very tall, with
the swell of the branching on the outer side of the slope so that the
peaks seem to point inwards to the mountain peak, like the lines
of the Parthenon, and the outline melodious and moving on many
focuses. – I wore my pagharee and turned it with harebells below

and gentians in two rows above like double pan-pipes. – In coming down we lost our way and each had a dangerous slide down the long wet grass of a steep slope.

1870

February. One day in the Long Retreat (which ended on Xmas Day) they were reading in the refectory Sister Emmerich's account of the Agony in the Garden and I suddenly began to cry and sob and could not stop. I put it down for this reason, that if I had been asked a minute beforehand I should have said that nothing of the sort was going to happen and even when it did I stood in a manner wondering at myself not seeing in my reason the traces of an adequate cause for such strong emotion – the traces of it I say because of course the cause in itself is adequate for the sorrow of a lifetime. I remember much the same thing on Maundy Thursday when the presanctified Host was carried to the sacristy. But neither the weight nor the stress of sorrow, that is to say of the thing which should cause sorrow, by themselves move us or bring the tears as a sharp knife does not cut for being pressed as long as it is pressed without any shaking of the hand but there is always one touch, something striking sideways and unlooked for, which in both cases undoes resistance and pierces, and this may be so delicate that the pathos seems to have gone directly to the body and cleared the understanding in its passage.

March 12. A fine sunset: . . . The next morning a heavy fall of snow. It tufted and toed the firs and yews and went on to load them till they were taxed beyond their spring. The limes, elms, and Turkey-oaks it crisped beautifully as with young leaf. Looking at the elms from underneath you saw every wave in every twig (become by this the wire-like stem to a finger of snow) and to the hangers and flying sprays it restored, to the eye, the inscapes they had lost. They were beautifully brought out against the sky, which was on one side dead blue, on the other washed with gold.

September 24. First saw the Northern Lights. . . . This busy working of nature wholly independent of the earth and seeming to go on in a strain of time not reckoned by our reckoning of days and years but simpler and as if correcting the preoccupation of the world by being preoccupied with and appealing to and dated to the day of judgment was like a new witness to God and filled me with delightful fear.

1871

End of March and beginning of April. – This is the time to study inscape in the spraying of trees, for the swelling buds carry them to a pitch which the eye could not else gather – for out of much much more, out of little not much, out of nothing nothing: in these sprays at all events there is a new world of inscape. The male ashes are very boldly jotted with the heads of the bloom which tuft the outer ends of the branches. The staff of each of these branches is closely knotted with the places where buds are or have been, so that it is something like a finger which has been tied up with string and keeps the marks. They are in knops of a pair, one on each side and the knops are set alternately, at crosses with the knops above and the knops below, the bud of course is a short smoke-black pointed nail-head or beak pieced of four lids or nippers. Below it, like hollow below the eye or the piece between the knuckle and the root of the nail, is a half-moon-shaped sill as if once chipped the wood and this gives the twig its quaining. . . .

April 22. But such a lovely damasking in the sky as today I never felt before. The blue was charged with same instress, the higher, zenith sky earnest and frowning, lower more light and sweet. High up again, breathing through woolly coats of cloud or on the quains and branches of the flying pieces it was the true exchange of crimson. . . .

May 9. This day and May 11 the bluebells in the little wood between the College and the highroad and in one of the Hurst Green cloughs. In the little wood / opposite the light / they stood in black-ish spreads or sheddings like the spots on a snake. The heads are then like thongs and solemn in grain and grape-colour. But in the clough / through the light / they came in falls of sky-colour washing the brows and slacks of the ground with vein-blue. . . . The blue-bells in your hand baffle you with their inscape. . . . With a shock of wet heads; the long stalks rub and click and flatten to a fan on one another like your fingers themselves would when you passed the palms hard across one another, making a brittle rub and jostle like the noise of a hurdle strained by leaning against; then there is the faint honey smell and in the mouth the sweet gum when you bite them. . . .

1872

March 13. After a time of trial and especially a morning in which I did not know which way to turn as the account of De Rancé's final conversion was being read at dinner the verse *Qui confidunt in D[omin]o sicut mons Sion*[14] which satisfied him and resolved him to enter his abbey of La Trappe by the mercy of God came strongly home to me too, so that I was choked for a little while and could not keep back my tears. . . .

July 19. The ovary of the blown foxglove surrounded by the green calyx is perhaps that conventional flower in pointed and other flo-riated work which I could not before identify. It might also be St. John's-wort.

Stepped into a barn of ours, a great shadowy barn, where the hay had been stacked on either side, and looking at the great rudely arched timberframes – principals (?) and tie-beams, which make them look like bold big A's with the cross-bar high up – I thought how sadly beauty of inscape was unknown and buried away from simple people and yet how near at hand it was if they had eyes to see it and it could be called out everywhere again. . . .

After the examinations we went for our holiday out to Douglas in the Isle of Man Aug. 3. At this time I had first begun to get hold of the copy of Scotus on the *Sentences* [15] in the Baddely [16] library and was flush with a new stroke of enthusiasm. It may come to nothing or it may be a mercy from God. But just then when I took in any inscape of the sky or sea I thought of Scotus.

October 5. A goldencrested wren had got into my room at night and circled round dazzled by the gaslight on the white ceiling; when caught even and put out it would come in again. Ruffling the crest which is mounted over the crown and eyes like beetlebrows, I smoothed and fingered the little orange and yellow feathers which are hidden in it. Next morning I found many of these about the room and enclosed them in a letter to Cyril on his wedding day.

1873

February 24. In the snow flat-topped hillocks and shoulders outlined with wavy edges, ridge below ridge, very like the grain of wood in line and in projection like relief maps. These the wind makes I think and of course drifts, which are in fact snow waves. The sharp nape of a drift is sometimes broken by slant flutes or channels. I think this must be when the wind after shaping the drift first has changed and cast waves in the body of the wave itself. All the world is full of inscape and chance left free to act falls into an order as well as purpose. . . .

April 8. The ash tree growing in the corner of the garden was felled. It was lopped first: I heard the sound and looking out and seeing it maimed there came at that moment a great pang and I wished to die and not to see the inscapes of the world destroyed any more.

July 22. Very hot, though the wind, which was south, dappled very sweetly on one's face and when I came out I seemed to put it on like a gown as a man puts on the shadow he walks into and hoods or hats himself with the shelter of a roof, a penthouse, or a copse of trees, I mean it rippled and fluttered like light linen, one could feel the folds and braids of it – and indeed a floating flag is like wind visible and what weeds are in a current; it gives it thew and fires it and bloods it in. – Thunderstorm in the evening, first booming in gong-sounds. . . .

September 18. . . . I had a nightmare that night. I thought something or someone leapt onto me, and held me quite fast: this I think woke me, so that after this I shall have had the use of reason. This first start is, I think, a nervous collapse of the same sort as when one is very tired and holding oneself at stress not to sleep yet / suddenly goes slack and seems to fall. . . . The feeling is terrible: the body no longer swayed as a piece by the nervous and muscular instress seems to fall in and hang like a dead weight on the chest. I cried on the holy name and by degrees recovered myself as I thought to do. It made me think that this was how the souls in hell wd. be imprisoned in their bodies. . . .

1874

July 23. . . . Our schools at Roehampton ended with two days of examination before St. Ignatius' feast the 31st. I was very tired and seemed deeply cast down till I had some kind words from the Provincial. Altogether perhaps my heart has never been so burdened and cast down as this year. The tax on my strength has been greater than I have felt before: at least now at Teignmouth I feel myself weak and can do little. But in all this our Lord goes His own way.

August 17. We went over to Ugbrooke at Lord Clifford's invitation. . . . As we drove home the stars came out thick: I leant back to look at them and my heart opening more than usual praised our Lord to and in whom all that beauty comes home.

PART III

from the Keep Carisbrooke
Castle.
July 25.

Reckoning with the Wreck

IN DECEMBER 1875, after seven years as a Jesuit, Gerard Manley Hopkins broke his poetic fast over a ship wrecked in a storm. This natural disaster introduced him to his new muse – God, Master of the Tide. "The Wreck of the Deutschland" embraces a rapture of tense adoration of a mastering Lord, who giveth and who taketh away. "The mystery must be instressed" when innocent victims are snatched from life by "he in three of the thunder throne." For Hopkins, "the God who is, is terrible." Both content and form of this poetic narrative reveal struggle – rapid and colliding sprung meters, rhymes, sounds, ideas – concluding with the poet's discovery of beauty and reconciliation in God's "lightning of fire hard-hurled." Ultimately, human language hovers on the inadequate to embody the experience of God. Confronted with theodicy – the question of why an omnipotent and supposedly beneficent God allows evil – Hopkins reached into the compendious treasury of his erudition and resurrected an ancient form. From the model of the Greek Pindaric ode he made a revolutionary work to mark the occasion of a martyrdom.

What does this ode do? Dedicated to the five nuns who drowned, Hopkins's "The Wreck of the Deutschland" first details his own conversion, and last, prays for the conversion of England. He is affected and even agitated by the martyrdom of the Catholic sisters. He identifies their number – "cinquefoil" – as coinciding with the five wounds of Christ. He also stresses the coincidence of the disaster with the Feast of the Immaculate Conception (December 8). But "The Wreck" is above all an ode to human redemption; the poet is the messenger; the tragedy takes place off-stage. Hopkins begins again in this masterpiece to write serious poetry after a long silence. The great editor of Hopkins's collected poems, W. H. Gardner, wrote: "Of Hopkins the poet much needs to be said; but we may introduce him by observing that he succeeded in breaking up, by a kind of creative violence, an outworn convention. He led poetry forward by taking it back – to its primal linguistic origins."[17]

The ancient Greek form, Welsh folklore, and a sixteenth-century handbook for making religious retreats all conspire in Hopkins's great ode to pull English poetry back, and then to catapult it forward.

My late beloved mentor, Professor William Alfred of Harvard University, introduced me to "The Wreck of the Deutschland" during my first year of college. One Friday night in his living room, Professor Alfred suggested that Gerard Manley Hopkins modeled "The Wreck" on the epinicion ode – a sixth-century BCE Greek semi-improvisational hymn which celebrated an athletic victory, slam-style. The epinicion ode sang (chorale or solo), danced, banged the drum, and plucked the lyre. Its earliest example (520 BCE) honored the victor in a boys' boxing match at Olympus.

Within a hundred years, Pindar became the most famous practitioner of this ode form. Professor Alfred pointed out that Hopkins, skilled in ancient Greek, would have found the epinicion/Pindaric ode an attractive form for the overture to the poetry of his own Olympic endeavor. Importantly, the Pindaric ode avoided standard Greek meter, sometimes varying beats.

Hopkins's ode varied beats explosively, to the wonder of all subsequent readers.

The disaster of a ship bearing religious exiles, wrecked by the random confluence of storm and sandbar and hull, rallied Hopkins's sense of his own internal catastrophe. Nine years after his controversial alliance with the ideologically dogmatic system of Roman Catholicism, seven years after foreswearing poetry and entering the tight constraint of the Jesuit order, Hopkins apparently perceived in the arbitrary drama of the wreck an opportunity to express a very great deal. The foundering of the ship *Deutschland* sparked in him a consideration of the problem of evil, of innocent suffering. Unlike the 1755 earthquake in Lisbon which threw the enlightened philosopher Voltaire into skeptical deism, the natural disaster which martyred the Franciscan sisters provoked Hopkins to encounter God powerfully and intimately. "The Wreck" more closely resembles an Olympic contest than a philosophical retreat. Indiscriminate suffering became coherent through the model of Pindaric poetry. Hopkins, encouraged by his superior to write "something," approached with enthusiasm this chance to commemorate not only the martyrdoms but his own sacrifice.

He got to work immediately. He asked his mother to send him newspaper clippings about the event. The tools he brought to the task included: demonstrated if outdated ability as a poet; extraordinary agility with Greek and Latin; the local Welsh language; impressions drawn from his father's maritime insurance business; an impulsive imagination constantly contending with Jesuit discipline; years of journal entries about the weather; personal experience with *The Spiritual Exercises of St. Ignatius Loyola;* and the desire to write.

The ode begins and ends in an ecstasy of energetic form, barely containing a violent drama. It opens with a *tmesis* – the

Greek device by which a sequence of words is ruptured by an intrusion. So the first line of the ode invokes Hopkins's muse: "Thou God." But Hopkins cleaves those two words with the lightning stroke of "mastering me." What kind of God? A mastering me God: "Thou mastering me / God!"

Norman White calls the ode "a poem about unmaking, unfathering, unchilding."[18] Occasionally the poet relaxes slightly: "I kiss my hand / To the stars, lovely-asunder." But mostly, Hopkins employs a huge arsenal of compounded language – "dappled-with-damson," "whirlwind-swivellèd," "lush-kept plush-capped," "flesh-burst," "cobbled foam-fleece" – retrieved or invented words – voel, flange, instress – and grand finale alexandrines at the ends of stanzas that sound like military tattoos – "The sour scythe cringe, the blear share come" and "Our héarts' charity's héarth's fire, our thóughts' chivalry's thróng's Lórd." No wonder, really, that the earliest audience for the poem – a few individual readers – said they would not read it again for any amount of money (Bridges) or that they found the poem, "while full of tremendous power," to be "grotesque" (a fellow Jesuit).

"The Wreck" consists of thirty-five eight-line stanzas, with metrical beats drumming over each set of eight, 2, 3, 4, 3, 5, 5, 4, 6. Part One, ten stanzas, provides an expressionistic autobiography of Hopkins's personal conversion, some of the lines paraphrasing *The Spiritual Exercises:* "I am an ulcer and abscess whence have issued so many sins." Part Two contains twenty-five stanzas, seven about the shipwreck off the southwest coast of England as reported in the *Times* of London on December 8, 1875; fourteen about the drownings; and four apostrophes to God the Master of the Tide, with a call for the conversion of England. The experimental ode is composed as a wild Greco-Welsh-Anglo-Saxon song and dance to drum and lyre with solo singer.

Hopkins first used his trademark "sprung rhythm" in "The Wreck." He said that he had "long had haunting" his ear "a new rhythm" which he "now realised on paper." Hopkins himself explains his use of rhythm in a short introduction to the poem to be used for possible publication:

> Be pleased, reader, since the rhythm in which the following poem is written is new, strongly to mark the beats of the measure according to the number belonging to each of the eight lines of the stanza, as the indentation guides the eye, namely two and three and four and three and five and five and four and six; not distinguishing the rhythm and rhyme, as some readers do, who treat poetry as if it were prose fantastically written to rule (which they mistakenly think the perfection of reading), but laying on the beat too much stress rather than too little, nor caring whether one, two, three, or more syllables go to a beat, that is to say, whether two or more beats follow running. . . . And so throughout let the stress be made to fetch out both the strength of the syllables and the meaning and feeling of the words.[19]

Helen Vendler, in her collection of essays *The Breaking of Style,* describes Hopkins's sprung rhythm as: "dangerous, irregular, and binary." Vendler further demonstrates that his choice of rhythm surpassed the aesthetic: it signaled a "breaking of style" from his pre-Jesuit poetry, each stanza providing a volatile phonetic event. His early, pre-Jesuit poems are neither sprung nor irregular. Vendler argues that a moral conversion must have occurred during his seven "silent" years as a Jesuit. By age thirty-one, he both tolerated and preferred irregularity and unpredictability. This tolerance may explain the difference between Hopkins's reaction to natural catastrophe and Voltaire's. In the second stanza of "The Wreck," Hopkins writes, "I did say yes / O at lightning and lashed rod." In this debut poem, he says "yes" to a difficult muse in a big way, with the energy of an acetylene torch. He does not retreat into agnosticism. Instead, he rises like a meteor to embrace the Master of the Tide.

Vendler suggests that the hammering stresses that mark his poetry after 1876 represent his perception of "a universe of continual irregular shocks . . . the impressions of a poet who receives the stimuli of daily life as a series of unforeseeable and unsettling assaults."[20] Indeed Hopkins "instresses" scapes inner and outer; he experiences life as stressed and stressful. But he lightens up by allowing musical variations and two-part fugues into the voice of the poetry. The rhythm of "The Wreck" is sometimes sprung, irregular, all force and beat – "The down-dugged ground-hugged grey" (stanza 26). Sometimes it piles up floating syllables, as in "Finger of a tender of, O of a feathery delicacy" (stanza 31) or "O Father, not under thy feathers . . ." (stanza 12). Musically, the ode varies between contrapuntal and experimental.

The day Hopkins read the news of the wreck of the Lloyd's liner *Deutschland* was the Feast of the Immaculate Conception. The shipwreck reckoned: five Franciscan nuns were exiled from Germany; as the ship sailed on stormy seas by England, it wrecked on a Kentish shoal; for thirty hours rescuers tried unsuccessfully to reach the dying passengers; fifty drowned, including the five nuns; one tall nun was heard to say "Christ come quickly" as a huge wave washed them overboard. Bad things happened to good people, and Hopkins composed an ode which conducted a heated if one-sided debate with the paradoxical Lord of living and dead: "Father and fondler of heart thou hast wrung / Hast thy dark descending and most art merciful then" (stanza 6). And then in stanza 22, "Five! The finding and sake / And cipher of suffering Christ. . . ." The five wounds of

Christ were impressed upon England, whether the poet liked it or not.

The ode considers not only the five women to whom it is dedicated, but also the Blessed Mother throughout. "The Wreck" presents a complex bouquet of allusions to Mary, to conception, to birth, on this double commemoration of the martyrdom of nuns and of Mary's feast: "Warm-laid-grave of a womb-life grey; / Manger, maiden's knee" (stanza 7); " – mother of being in me, heart" (stanza 18); "What was the feast followed the night / Thou hadst glory of this nun? – / Feast of the one woman without stain" (stanza 30); "Now burn, new born to the world, / Double-naturèd name, / The Heaven-flung, heart-fleshed maiden-furled / Miracle-in-Mary-of-flame" (stanza 34).

So, on that morning of December 8, 1875, near tears reading the front page of the newspaper, Hopkins himself conceived a miracle – with his own alchemy, he mixed Christian martyrdom, Greek prosody, the Ignatian exercises, a scientific eye, and the one-of-a-kind voice of a master singer long self-silenced. But none of the few who read the resulting poem liked it. It was passed over for publication in the Jesuit magazine, *The Month*. "I wish those nuns had stayed at home," was one response.

When, in 1918, Bridges published the limited (750 copies) first edition of Hopkins's poetry, his introduction referred to "The Wreck" as "the dragon folded in the gate to forbid all entrance." In his introduction to the fourth edition in 1967, W. H. Gardner more generously wrote that the poem "peals out like a massive overture to this man's too-brief opera." Only thirty-one and yet his sense of impotence and fragmentation is already burgeoning. In *The Linguistic Moment*, J. Hillis Miller perceives:

> The wreck is Hopkins's own, incarnated in his own flesh, blood, and self-taste, and it is at the same time the wreck he inherited

from his immediate predecessors in poetry. Hopkins's attempted repair of the disaster of Babel had long been preparing, for example in his early diaries and journals. It continues, of course in all the poems written after "The Wreck." Hopkins's poetic problem was to find a way to communicate the incommunicable. It was an attempted rescue of the self and of language through language. [21]

The twentieth-century American poet James Dickey asks, in his introduction to David Godine's fancy-print edition of "The Wreck," whether a simple calling out to the god in the machine is too complacent a solution to Hopkins's problem – the problem of being mastered by "Thou mastering me / God." Dickey answers his own question by claiming that nothing about the ode is complacent, because its language is so "desperately" original and risky. Dickey identifies "The Wreck" as the most impor-tant poem of the nineteenth and twentieth centuries, "breaking beach" with stunning new ideas of what poetry might achieve. I agree with Dickey, adding that the poet of "The Wreck" labors hard to bring nature into unity with God; this releases him as the poet he will be henceforth.

The Wreck of the Deutschland

To the happy memory of five Franciscan Nuns, exiles by the Falk Laws,[22] *drowned between midnight and morning of December 7, 1875*

Part the First

1

Thou mastering me
    God! giver of breath and bread;
  World's strand, sway of the sea;
    Lord of living and dead;
Thou hast bound bones and veins in me, fastened me flesh,
And after it almost unmade, what with dread,
    Thy doing: and dost thou touch me afresh?
Over again I feel thy finger and find thee.

2

I did say yes
    O at lightning and lashed rod;
  Thou heardst me truer than tongue confess
    Thy terror, O Christ, O God;
Thou knowest the walls, altar and hour and night:
The swoon of a heart that the sweep and the hurl of thee trod
    Hard down with a horror of height:
And the midriff astrain with leaning of, laced with fire of stress.

3

The frown of his face
Before me, the hurtle of hell
Behind, where, where was a, where was a place?
I whirled out wings that spell
And fled with a fling of the heart to the heart of the Host.
My heart, but you were dovewinged, I can tell,
Carrier-witted, I am bold to boast,
To flash from the flame to the flame then, tower from the grace to
the grace.

4

I am soft sift
In an hourglass – at the wall
Fast, but mined with a motion, a drift,
And it crowds and it combs to the fall;
I steady as a water in a well, to a poise, to a pane,
But roped with, always, all the way down from the tall
Fells or flanks of the voel, a vein
Of the gospel proffer, a pressure, a principle, Christ's gift.

5

I kiss my hand
To the stars, lovely-asunder
Starlight, wafting him out of it; and
Glow, glory in thunder;
Kiss my hand to the dappled-with-damson west:
Since, tho' he is under the world's splendour and wonder,
His mystery must be instressed, stressed;
For I greet him the days I meet him, and bless when I understand.

6

      Not out of his bliss
        Springs the stress felt
    Nor first from heaven (and few know this)
        Swings the stroke dealt –
Stroke and a stress that stars and storms deliver,
    That guilt is hushed by, hearts are flushed by and melt –
      But it rides time like riding a river
(And here the faithful waver, the faithless fable and miss).

7

      It dates from day
        Of his going in Galilee;
    Warm-laid grave of a womb-life grey;
        Manger, maiden's knee;
The dense and the driven Passion, and frightful sweat;
    Thence the discharge of it, there its swelling to be,
      Though felt before, though in high flood yet –
What none would have known of it, only the heart, being hard at
    bay,

8

      Is out with it! Oh,
        We lash with the best or worst
    Word last! How a lush-kept plush-capped sloe
        Will, mouthed to flesh-burst,
Gush! – flush the man, the being with it, sour or sweet,
    Brim, in a flash, full! – Hither then, last or first,
      To hero of Calvary, Christ,'s feet –
Never ask if meaning it, wanting it, warned of it – men go.

9

Be adored among men,
God, three-numberèd form;
Wring thy rebel, dogged in den,
Man's malice, with wrecking and storm.
Beyond saying sweet, past telling of tongue,
Thou art lightning and love, I found it, a winter and warm;
Father and fondler of heart thou hast wrung:
Hast thy dark descending and most art merciful then.

10

With an anvil-ding
And with fire in him forge thy will
Or rather, rather then, stealing as Spring
Through him, melt him but master him still:
Whether at once, as once at a crash Paul,
Or as Austin, a lingering-out sweet skill,
Make mercy in all of us, out of us all
Mastery, but be adored, but be adored King.

Part the Second

11

'Some find me a sword; some
The flange and the rail; flame,
Fang, or flood' goes Death on drum,
And storms bugle his fame.
But wé dream we are rooted in earth – Dust!
Flesh falls within sight of us, we, though our flower the same,
Wave with the meadow, forget that there must
The sour scythe cringe, and the blear share come.

12

On Saturday sailed from Bremen,
　　American-outward-bound,
　　Take settler and seamen, tell men with women,
　　　Two hundred souls in the round –
O Father, not under thy feathers nor ever as guessing
The goal was a shoal, of a fourth the doom to be drowned;
　　　Yet did the dark side of the bay of thy blessing
Not vault them, the million of rounds of thy mercy not reeve even
　them in?

13

Into the snows she sweeps
　　Hurling the haven behind,
　　The Deutschland, on Sunday; and so the sky keeps,
　　　For the infinite air is unkind,
And the sea flint-flake, black-backed in the regular blow,
Sitting Eastnortheast, in cursed quarter, the wind;
　　　Wiry and white-fiery and whirlwind-swivellèd snow
Spins to the widow-making unchilding unfathering deeps.

14

She drove in the dark to leeward,
　　She struck – not a reef or a rock
　　But the combs of a smother of sand: night drew her
　　　Dead to the Kentish Knock;
And she beat the bank down with her bows and the ride of her
　keel:
The breakers rolled on her beam with ruinous shock;
　　　And canvas and compass, the whorl and the wheel
Idle for ever to waft her or wind her with, these she endured.

15

Hope had grown grey hairs,
Hope had mourning on,
Trenched with tears, carved with cares,
Hope was twelve hours gone;
And frightful a nightfall folded rueful a day
Nor rescue, only rocket and lightship, shone,
And lives at last were washing away:
To the shrouds they took, – they shook in the hurling and horrible
airs.

16

One stirred from the rigging to save
The wild woman-kind below,
With a rope's end round the man, handy and brave –
He was pitched to his death at a blow,
For all his dreadnought breast and braids of thew:
They could tell him for hours, dandled the to and fro
Through the cobbled foam-fleece, what could he do
With the burl of the fountains of air, buck and the flood of the wave?

17

They fought with God's cold –
And they could not and fell to the deck
(Crushed them) or water (and drowned them) or rolled
With the sea-romp over the wreck.
Night roared, with the heart-break hearing a heart-broke
rabble,
The woman's wailing, the crying of child without check –
Till a lioness arose breasting the babble,
A prophetess towered in the tumult, a virginal tongue told.

18

Ah, touched in your bower of bone
Are you! turned for an exquisite smart,
Have you! make words break from me here all alone,
Do you! – mother of being in me, heart.
O unteachably after evil, but uttering truth,
Why, tears! is it? tears; such a melting, a madrigal start!
Never-eldering revel and river of youth,
What can it be, this glee? the good you have there of your own?

19

Sister, a sister calling
A master, her master and mine! –
And the inboard seas run swirling and hawling;
The rash smart sloggering brine
Blinds her; but she that weather sees one thing, one;
Has one fetch in her: she rears herself to divine
Ears, and the call of the tall nun
To the men in the tops and the tackle rode over the storm's
brawling.

20

She was first of a five and came
Of a coifèd sisterhood.
(O Deutschland, double a desperate name!
O world wide of its good!
But Gertrude, lily, and Luther, are two of a town,
Christ's lily and beast of the waste wood:
From life's dawn it is drawn down,
Abel is Cain's brother and breasts they have sucked the same.)

21

Loathed for a love men knew in them,
Banned by the land of their birth,
Rhine refused them. Thames would ruin them;
Surf, snow, river and earth
Gnashed: but thou art above, thou Orion of light;
Thy unchancelling poising palms were weighing the worth,
Thou martyr-master: in thy sight
Storm flakes were scroll-leaved flowers, lily showers – sweet heaven
was astrew in them.

22

Five! the finding and sake
And cipher of suffering Christ.
Mark, the mark is of man's make
And the word of it Sacrificed.
But he scores it in scarlet himself on his own bespoken,
Before-time-taken, dearest prizèd and priced –
Stigma, signal, cinquefoil token
For lettering of the lamb's fleece, ruddying of the rose-flake.

23

Joy fall to thee, father Francis,
Drawn to the Life that died;
With the gnarls of the nails in thee, niche of the lance, his
Lovescape crucified
And seal of his seraph-arrival! and these thy daughters
And five-livèd and leavèd favor and pride,
Are sisterly sealed in wild waters,
To bathe in his fall-gold mercies, to breathe in his all-fire glances.

24

      Away in the loveable west,
    On a pastoral forehead of Wales,
  I was under a roof here, I was at rest,
    And they the prey of the gales;
She to the black-about air, to the breaker, the thickly
Falling flakes, to the throng that catches and quails
  Was calling 'O Christ, Christ, come quickly':
The cross to her she calls Christ to her, christens her wild-worst
  Best.

25

     The majesty! what did she mean?
    Breathe, arch and original Breath.
  Is it love in her of the being as her lover had been?
    Breathe, body of lovely Death.
They were else-minded then, altogether, the men
Woke thee with a *we are perishing* in the weather of Gennesareth.
  Or is it that she cried for the crown then,
The keener to come at the comfort for feeling the combating keen?

26

     For how to the heart's cheering
    The down-dugged ground-hugged grey
  Hovers off, the jay-blue heavens appearing
    Of pied and peeled May!
Blue-beating and hoary-glow height; or night, still higher,
With belled fire and the moth-soft Milky Way,
  What by your measure is the heaven of desire,
The treasure never eyesight got, nor was ever guessed what for the
  hearing?

27

No, but it was not these.
The jading and jar of the cart,
Time's tasking, it is fathers that asking for ease
Of the sodden-with-its-sorrowing heart,
Not danger, electrical horror; then further it finds
The appealing of the Passion is tenderer in prayer apart:
Other, I gather, in measure her mind's
Burden, in wind's burly and beat of endragonèd seas.

28

But how shall I . . . make me room there:
Reach me a . . . Fancy, come faster –
Strike you the sight of it? look at it loom there,
Thing that she . . . there then! the Master,
Ipse, the only one, Christ, King, Head:
He was to cure the extremity where he had cast her;
Do, deal, lord it with living and dead;
Let him ride, her pride, in his triumph, despatch and have done
with his doom there.

29

Ah! there was a heart right!
There was single eye!
Read the unshapeable shock night
And knew the who and the why;
Wording it how but by him that present and past,
Heaven and earth are word of, worded by? –
The Simon Peter of a soul! to the blast
Tarpeian-fast, but a blown beacon of light.

30

Jesu, heart's light,
Jesu, maid's son,
What was the feast followed the night
Thou hadst glory of this nun? –
Feast of the one woman without stain.
For so conceivèd, so to conceive thee is done;
But here was heart-throe, birth of a brain,
Word, that heard and kept thee and uttered thee outright.

31

Well, she has thee for the pain, for the
Patience; but pity of the rest of them!
Heart, go and bleed at a bitterer vein for the
Comfortless unconfessed of them –
No not uncomforted: lovely-felicitous Providence
Finger of a tender of; O of a feathery delicacy, the breast of the
Maiden could obey so, be a bell to, ring of it, and
Startle the poor sheep back! is the shipwrack then a harvest,
does tempest carry the grain for thee?

32

I admire thee, master of the tides,
Of the Yore-flood, of the year's fall;
The recurb and the recovery of the gulf's sides,
The girth of it and the wharf of it and the wall;
Stanching, quenching ocean of a motionable mind;
Ground of being, and granite of it: past all
Grasp God, throned behind
Death with a sovereignty that heeds but hides, bodes but abides;

33

With a mercy that outrides
The all of water, an ark
For the listener; for the lingerer with a love glides
Lower than death and the dark;
A vein for the visiting of the past-prayer, pent in prison,
The-last-breath penitent spirits – the uttermost mark
Our passion-plungèd giant risen,
The Christ of the Father compassionate, fetched in the storm of his
strides.

34

Now burn, new born to the world,
Double-naturèd name,
The heaven-flung, heart-fleshed, maiden-furled
Miracle-in-Mary-of-flame,
Mid-numbered He in three of the thunder-throne!
Not a dooms-day dazzle in his coming nor dark as he came;
Kind, but royally reclaiming his own;
A released shower, let flash to the shire, not a lightning of fire
hard-hurled.

35

Dame, at our door
Drowned, and among our shoals,
Remember us in the roads, the heaven-haven of the Reward:
Our King back, oh, upon English souls!
Let him easter in us, be a dayspring to the dimness of us,
be a crimson-cresseted east,
More brightening her, rare-dear Britain, as his reign rolls,
Pride, rose, prince, hero of us, high-priest,
Our hearts' charity's hearth's fire, our thoughts' chivalry's throng's
Lord.

Letters

(1877–1878)

To Robert Bridges, August 21, 1877, from St. Beuno's

Dearest Bridges,

. . . Your parody reassures me about your understanding the meter. Only remark, as you say that there is no conceivable licence I shd. not be able to justify, that with all my licences, or rather laws, I am stricter than you and I might say than anybody I know. With the exception of the *Bremen* stanza,[23] which was, I think, the first written after 10 years' interval of silence, and before I had fixed my principles, my rhymes are rigidly good – to the ear – and such rhymes as *love* and *prove* I scout utterly. . . .

I do not of course claim to have invented *sprung rhythms* but only *sprung rhythm;* I mean that single lines and single instances of it are not uncommon in English and I have pointed them out in lecturing. . . . Moore has some which I cannot recall; there is one in *Grongar Hill;* and, not to speak of *Pom pom,* in Nursery Rhymes, Weather Saws, and Refrains they are very common – but what I do in the Deutschland, etc., is to enfranchise them as a regular and permanent principle of scansion.

There are no outriding feet in the Deutschland. An outriding foot is, by a sort of contradiction, a recognised extra-metrical effect; it is and it is not part of the meter; not part of it, not being counted, but part of it by producing a calculated effect which tells in the general success. But the long, e.g. seven-syllabled, feet of the Deutschland, are strictly metrical. Outriding feet belong to counterpointed verse, which supposes a well-known and unmistakeable or unforgettable standard rhythm: the Deutschland is not counterpointed; counterpoint is excluded by sprung rhythm. But in some of my sonnets I have mingled the two systems: this is the most delicate and difficult business of all. . . .

Why do I employ sprung rhythm at all? Because it is the nearest to the rhythm of prose, that is the native and natural rhythm of speech, the least forced, the most rhetorical and emphatic of all possible rhythms combining, as it seems to me, opposite and, one wd. have thought, incompatible excellences, markedness of rhythm – that is rhythm's self – and naturalness of expression – for why, if it is forcible in prose to say 'lashed : rod', am I obliged to weaken this in verse which ought to be stronger, not weaker, into 'láshed birch-ród' or something?

My verse is less to be read than heard, as I have told you before; it is oratorical, that is the rhythm is so. I think if you will study what I have here said you will be much more pleased with it and may I say? Converted to it.

You ask may you call it 'presumptious jugglery'. No, but only for this reason, that *presumptious* is not English.

I cannot think of altering anything. Why shd. I? I do not write for the public. You are my public and I hope to convert you.

You say you wd. not for any money read my poem again. Nevertheless I beg you will. Besides money, you know, there is love. If it is obscure do not bother yourself with the meaning but pay attention to the best and most intelligible stanzas, as the two last of each part and the narrative of the wreck. If you had done this you wd. have liked it better and sent me some serviceable criticisms, but now your criticism is of no use, being only a protest memorialising me against my whole policy and proceedings.

I may add for your greater interest and edification that what refers to myself in the poem is all strictly and literally true and did all occur; nothing is added for poetical padding.

Believe me your affectionate friend

Gerard M. Hopkins S.J.

To Robert Bridges, May 13, 1878, from Stonyhurst

Dearest Bridges, – Remark the above address. After July I expect to be stationed in town – 111 Mount Street, Grosvenor Square.

I hope your bad cold is gone . . . I enclose you my Eurydice, which the *Month* refused. It is my only copy. Write no bilgewater about it: I will presently tell you what that is and till then excuse the term. I must tell you I am sorry you never read the Deutschland again.

Granted that it needs study and is obscure, for indeed I was not over-desirous that the meaning of all should be quite clear, at least unmistakable, you might, without the effort that to make it all out would seem to have required, have nevertheless read it so that lines and stanzas should be left in the memory and superficial impressions deepened, and have liked some without exhausting all. I am sure I have read and enjoyed pages of poetry that way. Why, sometimes one enjoys and admires the very lines one cannot understand, as for instance 'If it were done when 'tis done' sqq., which is all obscure and disputed, though how fine it is everybody sees and nobody disputes. And so of many more passages in Shakespeare and others. Besides you would have got more weathered to the style and its features – not really odd. Now they say that vessels sailing from the port of London will take (perhaps it should be / used once to take) Thames water for the voyage: it was foul and stunk at first as the ship worked but by degrees casting its filth was in a few days very pure and sweet and wholesomer and better than any water in the world. However that may be, it is true to my purpose. When a new thing, such as my ventures in the Deutschland are, is presented us our first criticisms are not our truest, best, most homefelt, or most lasting but what come easiest on the instant. They are barbarous and like what the ignorant and the ruck say. This was so with you. The Deutschland on her first run worked very much and unsettled you, thickening and clouding your mind with vulgar mudbuttom and common sewage (I see that I am going it with the image) and just then unhappily you *drew off* your criticisms all stinking (a necessity now of the image) and bilgy, whereas if you had let your thoughts cast themselves they would have been clearer in themselves and more to my taste too. I did not heed them therefore, perceiving they were a first drawing-off. . . .

Your bodysnatch story is ghastly, but so are all bodysnatch stories. My grandfather was a surgeon, a fellow-student of Keats', and once conveyed a body through Plymouth at the risk of his own.

Believe me your affectionate friend

Gerard M. Hopkins S.J.

Dixon, a Church of England parish priest living in a village near Carlisle, had taught Hopkins at Highgate School. A classmate of Burne-Jones and Gabriel Rossetti, Dixon had taken Anglican orders on leaving Oxford and eventually become a published poet and church historian.

To R. W. Dixon, June 4, 1878, from Stonyhurst

Very Rev. Sir,
I take a liberty as a stranger in addressing you, nevertheless I did once have some slight acquaintance with you. You will not remember me but you will remember taking a mastership for some months at Highgate School, the Cholmeley School, where I then was. When you went away you gave, as I recollect, a copy of your book *Christ's Company* to one of the masters, a Mr. Law if I am not mistaken. By this means coming to know its name I was curious to read it, which when I went to Oxford I did. At first I was surprised at it, then pleased, at last I became so fond of it that I made it, so far as that could be, a part of my own mind. . . .

Gerard Hopkins

To R. W. Dixon, June 13, 1878, from Stonyhurst

. . . When I spoke of fame I was not thinking of the harm it does to men as artists: it may do them harm, as you say, but so, I think, may the want of it, if 'Fame is the spur that the clear spirit doth raise To shun delights and live laborious days'[24] – a spur very hard to find a substitute for or to do without. But I meant that it is a great danger in itself, as dangerous as wealth every bit, I should think, and as hard to enter the kingdom of heaven with. . . . And the world is full of things and events, phenomena of all sorts, that go without notice, go unwitnessed. I think you have felt this, for you say, I remember in one of the odes: 'What though the white clouds soar Unmarked from the horizon-shore?' or something like that. And if we regret this want of witness in brute nature much more in the things done with lost pains and disappointed hopes by man. But since there is always the risk of it, it is a great error of judgment to have lived for what may fail us. . . .

June 15 – This letter has run to a greater length than the little time at my disposal makes justifiable. – It is sad to think what disappointment must many times over have filled your heart for the darling children of your mind. Nevertheless fame whether won or lost is a thing which lies in the award of a random, reckless, incompetent, and unjust judge, the public, the multitude. The only just judge, the only just literary critic, is Christ, who prizes, is proud of, and admires, more than any man, more than the receiver himself can, the gifts of his own making. . . . Believe me, dear sir, very sincerely yours

Gerard Hopkins S.J.

To R. W. Dixon, October 5, 1878

Very Reverend and Dear Sir, . . . You ask, do I write verse myself. What I had written I burnt before I became a Jesuit and resolved to write no more, as not belonging to my profession, unless it were by the wish of my superiors; so for seven years I wrote nothing but two or three little presentation pieces which occasion called for. But when in the winter of '75 the *Deutschland* was wrecked in the mouth of the Thames and five Franciscan nuns, exiles from Germany by the Falk Laws, aboard of her were drowned I was affected by the account and happening to say so to my rector he said that he wished someone would write a poem on the subject. On this hint I set to work and, though my hand was out at first, produced one. . . . After writing this I held myself free to compose, but cannot find it in my conscience to spend time upon it; so I have done little and shall do less. But I wrote a shorter piece on the *Eurydice*, also in 'sprung rhythm', as I call it, but simpler, shorter, and without marks, and offered the *Month* that too, but they did not like it either. Also I have written some sonnets and a few other little things; some in sprung rhythm, with various other experiments – as 'outriding feet', that is parts of which do not count in the scanning (such as you find in Shakespeare's later plays, but as a licence, whereas mine are rather calculated effects); others in the ordinary scanning *counterpointed* (this is counterpoint: 'Hóme to his móther's hóuse *private* retúrned'[25] and 'Bút to vánquish by wísdom héllish wiles,[26] etc.); others, one or two, in common uncounterpointed rhythm. But even the impulse to write is wanting, for I have no thought of publishing . . . I hear confessions, preach, and so forth; when these are done I have still a good deal of time to myself, but I find I can do very little with it. . . .

 Believe me, dear Sir, very sincerely yours

Gerard Hopkins

To R. W. Dixon, May 12, 1879, from Oxford

. . . It was of course a very great pleasure to have so high an opinion expressed of my poems and by you.

 But for what concerns the notice you kindly offer to make of me in your forthcoming volume, it would not at all suit me. For this there are several reasons, any one sufficient; but it is enough to say now that 1) I have no thought of publishing until all circumstances favour, which I do not know that they ever will and it seems that one of them shd. be that the suggestion to publish shd. come from one of our own people; 2) to allow such a notice would be on my part a sort of insubordination to or double-dealing with my superiors. But nevertheless I sincerely thank you for you kind willingness to do me a service.

 The life I lead is liable to many mortifications but the want of fame as a poet is the least of them. I could wish, I allow, that my pieces could at some time become known but in some spontaneous way, so to speak, and without my forcing.

Believe me, with many thanks for the kindness which our letters always breathe, your sincere friend

Gerard M. Hopkins, S. J.

PART IV

Aug 27. Croydon

What I Do Is Me

IT MIGHT BE ACCURATE to say that Hopkins felt attracted to Duns Scotus's doctrine of "thisness," the "arch-especial" self of each thing, because he himself was so highly individual. At seminary, even amidst so distinctive an assembly as Jesuits, Hopkins struck others as an oddball, standing transfixed by the branchlike pattern of urine frozen on the wall of the outdoor latrine. Oddity, however, became the centerpiece of Hopkins's poetic focus, and within that focus he located the self-documenting presence of the person he called "Our Lord." Scotus affirmed Hopkins's tendency to take a simple assumption – the omnipresence of God, say – and specify it by embellishment, amplification, elaboration, and repeating patterns.

Hopkins's poems are actually not philosophically complex, just verbally complex. And Hopkins's self-imposed resistance to cliché and commonplace makes his work extraordinary: religious writers seem always to resort to the familiar, in an understandably insecure effort to make sense. For Hopkins, making sense is secondary, and if you take in – really take in – a line like "Stones ring; like each tucked string tells, each hung bell's / Bow swung finds tongue to fling out broad its name," it seems small-minded to request that this poet calm down, cut back, ease up.

In August 1874 Hopkins arrived at St. Beuno's College in Wales, where he would be happier than at any other time in his Jesuit career. He took a bath in the waters of the well of the seventh-century martyr, Saint Winifred. Hopkins considered the miraculous cures associated with these waters testimony to God's direct presence in nature. The rural landscape suited him far better than the urban slums to which his ministry would often lead him. It was here that he produced "The Wreck of the Deutschland" and a miraculous bundle of nature sonnets.

Throughout the next dozen years of unrecognized poetic genius, Hopkins would continue to rely on what he had learned from Scotus, who moved decisively from the ideal to the material without totally ditching the ideal. Although Hopkins ultimately would dismiss Keats for being too dreamy, he also learned something from Keats about the chameleon poet's talent for extinguishing the ego. In an ostensible irony, while avoiding egotism, Hopkins refined his concept of "selving" – by which a creature became itself – and rang it out in his gorgeous sonnet "As kingfishers catch fire, dragonflies draw flame": "Each mortal thing. . . . / goes itself; *myself* it speaks and spells, / Crying *Whát I dó is me: for that I came.*" Thus did Hopkins navigate the deep meanings of his objects – because of his minting of this idea of selving – "I am I because God wants me to be me." God resided at the fount of every detail. And for Hopkins, finally, ideal and detail, universal and particular, met in the penultimate line of "God's Grandeur": "The Holy Ghost over the bent / World broods. . . ."

At St. Beuno's, between February and October 1877, even while preparing for the theology exams which he would nearly fail in July, he wrote most of his extraordinary nature poems. On a day in February he wrote "God's Grandeur," declaring, "The world is charged with the grandeur of God" which "flames out," and "There lives the dearest freshness deep down things." In "Kingfishers," as in "God's Grandeur," the divine throws fire – but this time, it flames forth in the selving of each mortal thing.

In "Spring" – a common enough subject for poetic contemplation – Hopkins asks, "What is all this juice and all this joy?" God's presence shoots, rinses, rushes. A few months before his ordination he wrote "The Windhover," in which a bird becomes "dapple-dawn-drawn Falcon" and serves as an emblem for "Christ our Lord" when "Brute beauty and valor and act, oh, air, pride, plume, here / Buckle!" As with divine grandeur and with kingfishers, fire breaks and electrifies the poet. The sheer plod of quotidian work becomes "shine" in the sestet, and embers fall only to "gash gold vermilion." It was in high summer that he wrote his beloved curtal sonnet, ten and a half lines long, "Pied Beauty," which gives glory to God "for dappled things." Colors mix and vary and strike contrapuntal disharmonies; cows, trout, finches, all praise God in their sporting of traits contrary, strange, and original. And then, in "Hurrahing in Harvest," "Summer ends now . . . / I walk, I lift up, I lift up heart, eyes, / Down all that glory in the heavens to glean our Saviour." Finally, just before leaving Wales for good, he wrote "The Lantern out of Doors." In most of these sonnets, of course, euphoria fluctuates with corruption, Darwinian dustbins, crushing sadness, and ecological imbalance, and these bipolarities will dog Hopkins for the rest of his life.

After his third year of theologate, Hopkins scraped through the final exam. He passed, but did not do well enough to serve as a Jesuit rector or provincial; thus he would be consigned to common ministries for the rest of his life. This near-failure left him permanently disappointed. In his biography, *Gerard Manley Hopkins,* Paul Mariani agrees with other scholars that Hopkins, the brilliant Star of Balliol who left Oxford almost a dozen years before with a Double First, was graded harshly by his Jesuit examiners for preferring Scotus to Aquinas: "If the Thomistic way of understanding was via the species, Scotus was for individuation, the *haeceittas* or one-of-a kindness of experience."[27] Mariani adds to this suggestion the facts of Hopkins's chronic poor health (head colds, headaches, diarrhea, bleeding hemorrhoids, mental depression, exhaustion) and, of course, his personal eccentricity. These qualities would not suit an administrator in a rugged field of mission.

Deprived of the "long course," the fourth year of theologate which would have prepared him for leadership in the Society of Jesus, Hopkins was ordained a priest on September 23, 1877. He wrote one more sonnet while at St. Beuno's – "The Lantern out of Doors." This somber poem commemorates the eerie sight of a lantern carried through the dark: "Men go by me . . . / They rain against our much-thick and marsh air / Rich beams, till death or distance buys them quite. / Death or distance soon consumes them. . . ."

Hopkins left Wales on October 9, 1877. Immediately, he was assigned to assist in a parish and teach classics in a boys' school. Over the next two years he traveled to various assignments, but tended to find the work uncongenial. While serving at St. Aloysius in Oxford in 1879, however, he wrote a number of sonnets, including "Duns Scotus' Oxford" and "Henry Purcell." In both poems, Hopkins honored unsung English heroes – Scotus, whom he called "Of realty the rarest-veinèd unraveller"; and the seventeenth-century composer Henry Purcell, in whom Hopkins recognized not only *haecceitas,* but selving – "The poet wishes well to the divine genius of Purcell . . . [who] uttered in notes the very make and species of man. . . ."

Hopkins's ministry moved him to Liverpool, where he found the job so taxing that he fell into a very poor mental and physical state. Nevertheless, in 1880, he composed "Felix Randal," which comments on his priestly work with a dying farrier: "This seeing the sick endears them to us, us too it endears. . . . / When thou at the random grim forge, powerful amidst peers, / Didst fettle for the great grey drayhorse his bright and battering sandal!"

Alfred Thomas, author of *Hopkins the Jesuit,* writes of Hopkins at this time, "Liverpool he found hideous and his time there a nightmare almost from start to finish. Never before had he seen such stark and dire poverty, such misery and moral degradation. . . ."[28] Yet, in "Felix Randal" we don't encounter the moral agonies of the late sonnets, nor the ecstasies of the nature sonnets – rather we read a poem of consolation. Felix goes from big and handsome to sick and weak – and this "endears" Hopkins and Felix to each other. The suffering priest experiences an opening of love, which must reside at the heart of his vocation. In that year he also wrote "Spring and Fall" – "It is the blight man was born for / It is Margaret you mourn for" – destined to become his best known and most anthologized poem. In this poem, too, we read neither agony nor ecstasy, but rather, resignation to the human condition.

By the time Hopkins began to write his best poems, a new empiricism associated with Victorian science dominated the intellectual atmosphere. With this empiricism surely came an enhanced interest in, or even obsession with, specific details. Here Hopkins not only thrived but forged. Appropriating Scotus's teaching that individuality can be intuited, Hopkins promoted his own theories of instress and inscape: "instress being ultimately the stress of God's Will in and through all things. . . . Inscape a glimpse or a strain of universal harmony."

In *The Disappearance of God,* J. Hillis Miller examines the apparent departure of God from the Victorian world. The transcendent, the transgressive, the affirmation of self (Wordsworth), and the abnegation of self (Keats) spring up in God's place.[29] By the time Matthew Arnold publishes "Dover Beach," Victorians were experiencing not so much the Sea of Faith, "once, too at the full, and round earth's shore / . . . like the folds of a bright girdle furled" as its "melancholy, long, withdrawing roar." Hopkins, however, reintroduced the direct presence of God like a jolt of electricity into a closed system.

In fact, beginning with his amazing partial-year (1877) of writing nature sonnets in Wales, Hopkins's religious experience became inseparable from the poetry he produced. With "God's Grandeur" and the other Welsh sonnets, and most of his journal entries, Hopkins joins a poetic tradition that dates back at least to the biblical psalms – praising God for his creation. Here is the sestet of "Hurrahing":

> And the azurous hung hills are his world-wielding shoulder
>   Majestic – as a stallion stalwart, very-violet-sweet! –
>
> These things, these things were here and but the beholder
>   Wanting; which two when they once meet,
> The heart réars wíngs bold and bolder
>   And hurls for him, O half hurls earth for him off under his feet.

Nature thus is not merely sweet, not merely a useful companion to our "emotions recollected in tranquility,"[30] but the tangible proof of a system yearning only for a human consciousness to complete its electrical circuit. Every individual form is unique and none is dispensable, a theme climactic in the late, prodigious poem, "That Nature is a Heraclitean Fire and the Comfort of the Resurrection" – noise, joy, romping, tossed pillows of clouds, all summarized as the Greek philosopher Heraclitus would have done: "Million-fuelèd, nature's bonfire burns on."

Hopkins's dedication to rightly representing each thing as a self, with its own being and doing, combined with his habitual Jesuit dedication A.M.D.G. (*Ad Majorem Gloria Dei,* to the greater glory of God), meant that he could *not* digress from the world as God made it – not through a Wordsworthian egotistical sublimity, and not through a Keatsian drowsy numbness. Later in his life, Hopkins would describe his own preference for "an austerer utterance in art," as a reaction against Keats's luxury and sensualism. To deviate from precise selfhood would have bestowed upon Hopkins the nihilism of art for art's sake; it would have left him drifting away from the redemptive meaning he sought by becoming a Catholic.

Hopkins never represented an archetype or universal, but only individuals. He selected individuals as descriptors for how he sought patterning. Through networking, through recurrence, things revealed meaning. Otherwise, life on earth really would be random, really would be just one damned thing after another. Hopkins studied Darwin, recognizing that laws of nature rescue details from chaos and randomness. Yet in "the widow-making unchilding unfathering" capacity of nature, wherein prayers seem to go ignored – here Hopkins encountered God, too. Like Darwin, he rejected the conventional Victorian view of creation as totally comprehensible.

He focused hard on detecting a pattern of integration between individuals and an intelligent universe, seeing clouds as "shires" and observing them "quaining and squaring." He wrote about the visuals of things such as clouds like none other – with more verbal originality not to say *haecceitas* than anyone – proving that despite his early passions for drawing and music, Hopkins was vocationally adapted to the medium of language. "The Windhover," which Hopkins thought his own best poem, implies the question, can I selve too? The poem offers gliding and riding and galling and gashing, but only out of the poet's own modest service, out of "sheer plod," will come "shine." As in "God's Grandeur," the world over which Hopkins's falcon glides ("in his riding / Of the rolling level underneath him steady air . . .") is charged, not only with verbal force, but with breaking fire, heavy wind, shining, and burning which transform blue-bleak to gold-vermilion.

The energy of the windhover's world charges upward. Hopkins finds new language to describe a bird flying overhead. His method employs the basic materials of short words, drumming rhythms, alliterations, compressions, French chivalry, and Anglo-Saxon economies. He tolerates no metrical filler words. He imagines upward energy released when the Incarnation discharges into nature, and when the divine presence discharges into a wafer of bread. "This morning morning's minion": it actually sounds like the bird's wings overhead.

Hopkins constantly reminds his readers that the earth is the body of God. In his nature sonnets, the sensuous poet collides with the religious master, usually in the first eight lines, and the religious master is then released to spend the six final lines rhapsodizing about God. Until he was in his thirties, Hopkins was always down on his knees with a sketchbook or journal, squinting at something tiny that disclosed the Big Picture. And then, when he left his notebooks for writing – however rarely – poetry, every poem contained a collision. In the octet of each of his sonnets, we meet nature interacting with humanity; in the sestet, we meet God. Between the octet and the sestet, we encounter the volta – a turning, a white space – and in this sacred space occurs a transformation in every sonnet Hopkins wrote.

Poems

(1877–1882)

God's Grandeur

The world is charged with the grandeur of God.
    It will flame out, like shining from shook foil;
    It gathers to a greatness, like the ooze of oil
Crushed. Why do men then now not reck his rod?
Generations have trod, have trod, have trod;
    And all is seared with trade; bleared, smeared with toil;
    And wears man's smudge and shares man's smell: the soil
Is bare now, nor can foot feel, being shod.

And for all this, nature is never spent;
    There lives the dearest freshness deep down things;
And though the last lights off the black West went
    Oh, morning, at the brown brink eastward, springs –
Because the Holy Ghost over the bent
    World broods with warm breast and with ah! bright wings.

The Starlight Night

Look at the stars! look, look up at the skies!
　　O look at all the fire-folk sitting in the air!
　　The bright boroughs, the circle-citadels there!
Down in dim woods the diamond delves! the elves'-eyes!
The grey lawns cold where gold, where quickgold lies!
　　Wind-beat whitebeam! airy abeles set on a flare!
　　Flake-doves sent floating forth at a farmyard scare! –
Ah well! it is all a purchase, all is a prize.

Buy then! bid then! – What? – Prayer, patience, alms, vows.
Look, look: a May-mess, like on orchard boughs!
　　Look! March-bloom, like on mealed-with-yellow sallows!
These are indeed the barn; withindoors house
The shocks. This piece-bright paling shuts the spouse
　　Christ home, Christ and his mother and all his hallows.

Spring

Nothing is so beautiful as spring –
　　When weeds, in wheels, shoot long and lovely and lush;
　　Thrush's eggs look little low heavens, and thrush
Through the echoing timber does so rinse and wring
The ear, it strikes like lightnings to hear him sing;
　　The glassy peartree leaves and blooms, they brush
　　The descending blue; that blue is all in a rush
With richness; the racing lambs too have fair their fling.

What is all this juice and all this joy?
　　A strain of the earth's sweet being in the beginning
In Eden garden. – Have, get, before it cloy,
　　Before it cloud, Christ, lord, and sour with sinning,
Innocent mind and Mayday in girl and boy,
　　Most, O maid's child, thy choice and worthy the winning.

The Sea and the Skylark

On ear and ear two noises too old to end
   Trench – right, the tide that ramps against the shore;
   With a flood or a fall, low lull-off or all roar,
Frequenting there while moon shall wear and wend.

Left hand, off land, I hear the lark ascend,
   His rash-fresh re-winded new-skeinèd score
   In crisps of curl off wild winch whirl, and pour
And pelt music, till none's to spill nor spend.

How these two shame this shallow and frail town!
   How ring right out our sordid turbid time,
Being pure! We, life's pride and cared-for crown,

   Have lost that cheer and charm of earth's past prime:
Our make and making break, are breaking, down
   To man's last dust, drain fast towards man's first slime.

In the Valley of the Elwy

I remember a house where all were good
    To me, God knows, deserving no such thing:
    Comforting smell breathed at very entering,
Fetched fresh, as I suppose, off some sweet wood.
That cordial air made those kind people a hood
    All over, as a bevy of eggs the mothering wing
    Will, or mild nights the new morsels of spring:
Why, it seemed of course; seemed of right it should.

Lovely the woods, waters, meadows, combes, vales,
All the air things wear that build this world of Wales;
    Only the inmate does not correspond:
God, lover of souls, swaying considerate scales,
Complete thy creature dear O where it fails,
    Being mighty a master, being a father and fond.

The Windhover:
To Christ our Lord

I caught this morning morning's minion, king-
   dom of daylight's dauphin, dapple-dawn-drawn Falcon,
     in his riding
Of the rolling level underneath him steady air, and striding
High there, how he rung upon the rein of a wimpling wing
In his ecstasy! then off, off forth on swing,
   As a skate's heel sweeps smooth on a bow-bend: the hurl and
     gliding
Rebuffed the big wind. My heart in hiding
Stirred for a bird, – the achieve of, the mastery of the thing!

Brute beauty and valour and act, oh, air, pride, plume, here
   Buckle! AND the fire that breaks from thee then, a billion
Times told lovelier, more dangerous, O my chevalier!

   No wonder of it: shéer plód makes plough down sillion
Shine, and blue-bleak embers, ah my dear,
   Fall, gall themselves, and gash gold-vermillion.

Pied Beauty

Glory be to God for dappled things –
    For skies of couple-colour as a brinded cow;
        For rose-moles all in stipple upon trout that swim;
Fresh-firecoal chestnut-falls; finches' wings;
    Landscape plotted and pieced – fold, fallow, and plough;
        And áll trádes, their gear and tackle and trim.

All things counter, original, spare, strange;
    Whatever is fickle, freckled (who knows how?)
        With swift, slow; sweet, sour; adazzle, dim;
He fathers-forth whose beauty is past change:
        Praise him.

The Caged Skylark

As a dare-gale skylark scanted in a dull cage
    Man's mounting spirit in his bone-house, mean house,
        dwells –
    That bird beyond the remembering his free fells;
This in drudgery, day-labouring-out life's age.

Though aloft on turf or perch or poor low stage,
    Both sing sometímes the sweetest, sweetest spells,
    Yet both droop deadly sómetimes in their cells
Or wring their barriers in bursts of fear or rage.

Not that the sweet-fowl, song-fowl, needs no rest –
Why, hear him, hear him babble and drop down to his nest,
    But his own nest, wild nest, no prison.

Man's spirit will be flesh-bound when found at best,
But uncumbered: meadow-down is not distressed
    For a rainbow footing it nor he for his bónes rísen.

Hurrahing in Harvest

Summer ends now; now, barbarous in beauty, the stooks rise
    Around; up above, what wind-walks! what lovely behaviour
    Of silk-sack clouds! has wilder, wilful-wavier
Meal-drift moulded ever and melted across skies?

I walk, I lift up, I lift up heart, eyes,
    Down all that glory in the heavens to glean our Saviour;
    And, éyes, heárt, what looks, what lips yet gave you a
Rapturous love's greeting of realer, of rounder replies?

And the azurous hung hills are his world-wielding shoulder
    Majestic – as a stallion stalwart, very-violet-sweet! –
These things, these things were here and but the beholder
    Wanting; which two when they once meet,
The heart rears wings bold and bolder
    And hurls for him, O half hurls earth for him off under his feet.

The Lantern out of Doors

Sometimes a lantern moves along the night,
   That interests our eyes. And who goes there?
   I think; where from and bound, I wonder, where,
With, all down darkness wide, his wading light?

Men go by me whom either beauty bright
   In mould or mind or what not else makes rare:
   They rain against our much-thick and marsh air
Rich beams, till death or distance buys them quite.

Death or distance soon consumes them: wind
   What most I may eye after, be in at the end
I cannot, and out of sight is out of mind.

Christ minds; Christ's interest, what to avow or amend
   There, éyes them, heart wánts, care haúnts, foot fóllows kínd,
Their ránsom, théir rescue, ánd first, fást, last friénd.

The Loss of the Eurydice

Foundered March 24, 1878

1

The Eurydice – it concerned thee, O Lord:
Three hundred souls, O alas! on board,
    Some asleep unawakened, all un-
warned, eleven fathoms fallen

2

Where she foundered! One stroke
Felled and furled them, the hearts of oak!
    And flockbells off the aerial
Downs' forefalls beat to the burial.

3

For did she pride her, freighted fully, on
Bounden bales or a hoard of bullion? –
    Precious passing measure,
Lads and men her lade and treasure.

4

She had come from a cruise, training seamen –
Men, boldboys soon to be men:
    Must it, worst weather,
Blast bole and bloom together?

5

No Atlantic squall overwrought her
Or rearing billow of the Biscay water:
    Home was hard at hand
And the blow bore from land.

6

And you were a liar, O blue March day.
Bright sun lanced fire in the heavenly bay;
    But what black Boreas wrecked her? he
Came equipped, deadly-electric,

7

A beetling baldbright cloud thorough England
Riding: there did storms not mingle? and
    Hailropes hustle and grind their
Heavengravel? wolfsnow, worlds of it, wind there?

8

Now Carisbrook keep goes under in gloom;
Now it overvaults Appledurcombe;
    Now near by Ventnor town
It hurls, hurls off Boniface Down.

9

Too proud, too proud, what a press she bore!
Royal, and all her royals wore.
    Sharp with her, shorten sail!
Too late; lost; gone with the gale.

10

This was that fell capsize,
As half she had righted and hoped to rise
    Death teeming in by her portholes
Raced down decks, round messes of mortals.

11

Then a lurch forward, frigate and men;
'All hands for themselves' the cry ran then;
   But she who had housed them thither
Was around them, bound them or wound them with her.

12

Marcus Hare, high her captain,
Kept to her – care-drowned and wrapped in
   Cheer's death, would follow
His charge through the champ-white water-in-a-wallow,

13

All under Channel to bury in a beach her
Cheeks: Right, rude of feature,
   He thought he heard say
'Her commander! and thou too, and thou this way.'

14

It is even seen, time's something server,
In mankind's medley a duty-swerver,
   At downright 'No or yes?'
Doffs all, drives full for righteousness.

15

Sydney Fletcher, Bristol-bred,
(Low lie his mates now on watery bed)
   Takes to the seas and snows
As sheer down the ship goes.

16

Now her afterdraft gullies him too down;
Now he wrings for breath with the deathgush brown;
    Till a lifebelt and God's will
Lend him a lift from the sea-swill.

17

Now he shoots short up to the round air;
Now he gasps, now he gazes everywhere;
    But his eye no cliff, no coast or
Mark makes in the riveling snowstorm.

18

Him, after an hour of wintry waves,
A schooner sights, with another, and saves,
    And he boards her in Oh! such joy
He has lost count what came next, poor boy. –

19

They say who saw one sea-corpse cold
He was all of lovely manly mould,
    Every inch a tar,
Of the best we boast our sailors are.

20

Look, foot to forelock, how all things suit! he
Is strung by duty, is strained to beauty,
    And brown-as-dawning-skinned
With brine and shine and whirling wind.

21

O his nimble finger, his gnarled grip!
Leagues, leagues of seamanship
   Slumber in these forsaken
Bones, this sinew, and will not waken.

22

He was but one like thousands more,
Day and night I deplore
   My people and born own nation,
Fast foundering own generation.

23

I might let bygones be – our curse
Of ruinous shrine no hand or, worse,
   Robbery's hand is busy to
Dress, hoar-hallowèd shrines unvisited;

24

Only the breathing temple and fleet
Life, this wildworth blown so sweet,
   These daredeaths, ay this crew, in
Unchrist, all rolled in ruin –

25

Deeply surely I need to deplore it,
Wondering why my master bore it,
   The riving off that race
So at home, time was, to his truth and grace

26

That a starlight-wender of ours would say
The marvelous Milk was Walsingham Way
   And one – but let be, let be:
More, more than was will yet be. –

27

O well wept, mother have lost son;
Wept, wife; wept, sweetheart would be one:
   Though grief yield them no good
Yet shed what tears sad truelove should.

28

But to Christ lord of thunder
Crouch; lay knee by earth low under:
   'Holiest, loveliest, bravest,
Save my hero, O Hero savest.

29

And the prayer thou hearst me making
Have, at the awful overtaking,
   Heard; have heard and granted
Grace that day grace was wanted.'

30

Not that hell knows redeeming,
But for souls sunk in seeming
   Fresh, till doomfire burn all,
Prayer shall fetch pity eternal.

The May Magnificat

May is Mary's month, and I
Muse at that and wonder why:
    Her feasts follow reason,
    Dated due to season –

Candlemas, Lady Day;
But the Lady Month, May,
    Why fasten that upon her,
    With a feasting in her honour?

Is it only its being brighter
Than the most are must delight her?
    Is it opportunest
    And flowers finds soonest?

Ask of her, the mighty mother:
Her reply puts this other
    Question: What is Spring? –
    Growth in every thing –

Flesh and fleece, fur and feather,
Grass and greenworld all together;
    Star-eyed strawberry-breasted
    Throstle above her nested

Cluster of bugle blue eggs thin
Forms and warms the life within;
    And bird and blossom swell
    In sod or sheath or shell.

All things rising, all things sizing
Mary sees, sympathising
   With that world of good,
   Nature's motherhood.

Their magnifying of each its kind
With delight calls to mind
   How she did in her stored
   Magnify the Lord.

Well but there was more than this:
Spring's universal bliss
   Much, had much to say
   To offering Mary May.

When drop-of-blood-and-foam-dapple
Bloom lights the orchard-apple
   And thicket and thorp are merry
   With silver-surfèd cherry

And azuring-over greybell makes
Wood banks and brakes wash wet like lakes
   And magic cuckoocall
   Caps, clears, and clinches all –

This ecstasy all through mothering earth
Tells Mary her mirth till Christ's birth
   To remember and exultation
   In God who was her salvation.

Duns Scotus' Oxford

Towery city and branchy between towers;
Cuckoo-echoing, bell-swarmèd, lark-charmèd, rook-racked,
    river-rounded;
The dapple-eared lily below thee; that country and town did
Once encounter in, here coped and poisèd powers;

Thou hast a base and brickish skirt there, sours
That neighbor-nature thy grey beauty is grounded
Best in; graceless growth, thou hast confounded
Rural rural keeping – folk, flocks, and flowers.

Yet ah! this air I gather and I release
He lived on; these weeds and waters, these walls are what
He haunted who of all men most sways my spirits to peace;

Of realty the rarest-veinèd unraveller; a not
Rivalled insight, be rival Italy or Greece;
Who fired France for Mary without spot.

Binsey Poplars

felled 1879

My aspens dear, whose airy cages quelled,
Quelled or quenched in leaves the leaping sun,
All felled, felled, are all felled;
    Of a fresh and following folded rank
        Not spared, not one
        That dandled a sandaled
      Shadow that swam or sank
On meadow and river and wind-wandering weed-winding bank.

  O if we but knew what we do
      When we delve or hew –
    Hack and rack the growing green!
      Since country is so tender
    To touch, her being só slender,
    That, like this sleek and seeing ball
    But a prick will make no eye at all,
    Where we, even where we mean
        To mend her we end her,
      When we hew or delve:
After-comers cannot guess the beauty been.
    Ten or twelve, only ten or twelve
      Strokes of havoc únselve
        The sweet especial scene,
      Rural scene, a rural scene,
      Sweet especial rural scene.

Henry Purcell

*The poet wishes well to the divine genius of Purcell and praises him
that, whereas other musicians have given utterance to the moods
of man's mind, he has, beyond that, uttered in notes the very
make and species of man as created both in him and in all men
generally.*

Have fair fallen, O fair, fair have fallen, so dear
To me, so arch-especial a spirit as heaves in Henry Purcell,
An age is now since passed, since parted; with the reversal
Of the outward sentence low lays him, listed to a heresy, here.

Not mood in him nor meaning, proud fire or sacred fear,
Or love or pity or all that sweet notes not his might nursle:
It is the forgèd feature finds me; it is the rehearsal
Of own, of abrupt self there so thrusts on, so throngs the ear.

Let him oh! with his air of angels then lift me, lay me!
   only I'll
Have an eye to the sakes of him, quaint moonmarks, to his pelted
   plumage under
Wings: so some great stormfowl, whenever he has walked
   his while

The thunder-purple seabeach plumèd purple-of-thunder,
If a wuthering of his palmy snow-pinions scatter a colossal smile
Off him, but meaning motion fans fresh our wits with wonder.

The Candle Indoors

Some candle clear burns somewhere I come by.
I muse at how its being puts blissful back
With yellowy moisture mild night's blear-all black,
Or to-fro tender trambeams truckle at the eye.
By that window what task what fingers ply,
I plod wondering, a-wanting, just for lack
Of answer the eagerer a-wanting Jessy or Jack
There God to aggrándise, God to glorify. –

Come you indoors, come home; your fading fire
Mend first and vital candle in close heart's vault:
You there are master, do your own desire;
What hinders? Are you beam-blind, yet to a fault
In a neighbor deft-handed? are you that liar
And, cast by conscience out, spendsavor salt?

The Bugler's First Communion

A bugler boy from barrack (it is over the hill
There) – boy bugler, born, he tells me, of Irish
    Mother to an English sire (he
Shares their best gifts surely, fall how things will),

This very very day came down to us after a boon he on
My late being there begged of me, overflowing
    Boon in my bestowing,
Came, I say, this day to it – to a First Communion.

Here he knelt then ín regimental red.
Forth Christ from cupboard fetched, how fain I of feet
    To his youngster take his treat!
Low-latched in leaf-light housel his too huge godhead.

There! and your sweetest sendings, ah divine,
By it, heavens, befall him! as a heart Christ's darling, dauntless;
    Tongue true, vaunt- and tauntless;
Breathing bloom of a chastity in mansex fine.

Frowning and forefending angel-warder
Squander the hell-rook ranks sally to molest him;
    March, kind comrade, abreast him;
Dress his days to a dexterous and starlight order.

How it dóes my heart good, visiting at that bleak hill,
When limber liquid youth, that to all I teach
    Yields tender as a pushed peach,
Hies headstrong to its wellbeing of a self-wise self-will!

Then though I should tread tufts of consolation
Dáys áfter, só I in a sort deserve to
    And do serve God to serve to
Just such slips of soldiery Christ's royal ration.

Nothing élse is like it, no, not all so strains
Us: fresh youth fretted in a bloomfall all portending
    That sweet's sweeter ending;
Realm both Christ is heir to and thére réigns.

O now well work that sealing sacred ointment!
O for now charms, arms, what bans off bad
    And locks love ever in a lad!
Let mé though see no more of him, and not disappointment

Those sweet hopes quell whose least me quickenings lift,
In scarlet or somewhere of some day seeing
    That brow and bead of being,
An our day's God's own Galahad. Though this child's drift

Seems by a divíne doom chánnelled, nor do I cry
Disaster there; but may he not rankle and roam
    In backwheels though bound home? –
That left to the Lord of the Eucharist, I here lie by;

Recorded only, I have put my lips on pleas
Would brandle adamantine heaven with ride and jar, did
    Prayer go disregarded:
Forward-like, but however, and like favorable heaven heard these.

Peace

When will you ever, Peace, wild wooddove, shy wings shut,
Your round me roaming end, and under be my boughs?
When, when, Peace, will you, Peace? I'll not play hypocrite
To own my heart: I yield you do come sometimes; but
That piecemeal peace is poor peace. What pure peace allows
Alarms of wars, the daunting wars, the death of it?

O surely, reaving Peace, my Lord should leave in lieu
Some good! And so he does leave Patience exquisite,
That plumes to Peace thereafter. And when Peace here does house
He comes with work to do, he does not come to coo,
    He comes to brood and sit.

Felix Randal

Felix Randal the farrier, O he is dead then? my duty all ended,
Who have watched his mould of man, big-boned and hardy-
    handsome
Pining, pining, till time when reason rambled in it and some
Fatal four disorders, fleshed there, all contended?

Sickness broke him. Impatient he cursed at first, but mended
Being anointed and all; though a heavenlier heart began some
Months earlier, since I had our sweet reprieve and ransom
Tendered to him. Ah well, God rest him all road ever he
    offended!

This seeing the sick endears them to us, us too it endears.
My tongue had taught thee comfort, touch had quenched thy
    tears,
Thy tears that touched my heart, child, Felix, poor Felix Randal;

How far from then forethought of, all thy more boisterous years,
When thou at the random grim forge, powerful amidst peers,
Didst fettle for the great grey drayhorse his bright and battering
    sandal!

Spring and Fall

to a young child

Márgarét, áre you gríeving
Over Goldengrove unleaving?
Leáves, líke the things of man, you
With your fresh thoughts care for, can you?
Áh! ás the heart grows older
It will come to such sights colder
By and by, nor spare a sigh
Though worlds of wanwood leafmeal lie;
And yet you wíll weep and know why.
Now no matter, child, the name:
Sórrow's spríngs áre the same.
Nor mouth had, no nor mind, expressed
What heart heard of, ghost guessed:
It ís the blight man was born for,
It is Margaret you mourn for.

As kingfishers catch fire, dragonflies dráw fláme

As kingfishers catch fire, dragonflies dráw fláme;
As tumbled over rim in roundy wells
Stones ring; like each tucked string tells, each hung bell's
Bow swung finds tongue to fling out broad its name;
Each mortal thing does one thing and the same:
Deals out that being indoors each one dwells;
Selves – goes itself; *myself* it speaks and spells,
Crying *Whát I do is me: for that I came.*

Í say móre: the just man justices;
Kéeps gráce: thát keeps all his goings graces;
Acts in God's eye what in God's eye he is –
Chríst – for Christ plays in ten thousand places,
Lovely in limbs, and lovely in eyes not his
To the Father through the features of men's faces.

Inversnaid

This darksome burn, horseback brown,
His rollrock highroad roaring down,
In coop and in comb the fleece of his foam
Flutes and low to the lake falls home.

A windpuff-bonnet of fáwn-fróth
Turns and twindles over the broth
Of a pool so pitchblack, féll-frówning,
It rounds and rounds Despair to drowning.

Degged with dew, dappled with dew
Are the groins of the braes that the brook treads through,
Wiry heathpacks, flitches of fern,
And the beadbonny ash that sits over the burn.

What would the world be, once bereft
Of wet and of wildness? Let them be left,
O let them be left, wildness and wet;
Long live the weeds and the wilderness yet.

The Leaden Echo and the Golden Echo

Maidens' song from St. Winefred's Well

The Leaden Echo

How to kéep – is there ány any, is there none such, nowhere
    known some, bow or brooch or braid or brace, láce, latch
    or catch or key to keep
Back beauty, keep it, beauty, beauty, beauty, . . . from vanishing
    away?
Ó is there no frowning of these wrinkles, rankèd wrinkles deep,
Dówn? no waving off of these most mournful messengers, still
    messengers, sad and stealing messengers of grey?
No there's none, there's none, O no there's none,
Nor can you long be, what you now are, called fair,
Do what you may do, what, do what you may,
And wisdom is early to despair:
Be beginning; since, no, nothing can be done
To keep at bay
Age and age's evils, hoar hair,
Ruck and wrinkle, drooping, dying, death's worst, winding
    sheets, tombs and worms and tumbling to decay;
So be beginning, be beginning to despair.
O there's none; no no no there's none:
Be beginning to despair, to despair,
Despair, despair, despair, despair.

The Golden Echo

    Spare!
There ís one, yes I have one (Hush there!);
Only not within seeing of the sun,
Not within the singeing of the strong sun,
Tall sun's tingeing, or treacherous the tainting of the earth's air,
Somewhere elsewhere there is ah well where! one,

One. Yes I can tell such a key, I do know such a place,
Where whatever's prized and passes of us, everything that's
    fresh and fast flying of us, seems to us sweet of us and
    swiftly away with, done away with, undone,
Undone, done with, soon done with, and yet dearly and
    dangerously sweet
Of us, the wimpled-water-dimpled, not-by-morning-matchèd
    face,
The flower of beauty, fleece of beauty, too too apt to, ah! to fleet,
Never fleets móre, fastened with the tenderest truth
To its own best being and its loveliness of youth: it is an everlast-
    ingness of, O it is an all youth!
Come then, your ways and airs and looks, locks, maiden gear,
    gallantry and gaiety and grace,
Winning ways, airs innocent, maiden manners, sweet looks,
    loose locks, long locks, lovelocks, gaygear, going gallant,
        girlgrace –
Resign them, sign them, seal them, send them, motion them with
    breath,
And with sighs soaring, soaring síghs deliver
Them; beauty-in-the-ghost, deliver it, early now, long before
    death
Give beauty back, beauty, beauty, beauty, back to God, beauty's
    self and beauty's giver.
See; not a hair is, not an eyelash, not the least lash lost; every hair
Is, hair of the head, numbered.
Nay, what we had lighthanded left in surly the mere mould
Will have waked and have waxed and have walked with the wind
    what while we slept,
This side, that side hurling a heavyheaded hundredfold
What while we, while we slumbered.
O then, weary then whý should we tread? O why are we so
    haggard at the heart, so care-coiled, care-killed, so fagged, so
    fashed, so cogged, so cumbered,

When the thing we freely fórfeit is kept with fonder a care,
Fonder a care kept than we could have kept it, kept
Far with fonder a care (and we, we should have lost it) finer,
    fonder
A care kept. – Where kept? Do but tell us where kept, where. –
Yonder. – What high as that! We follow, now we follow. –
    Yonder, yes yonder, yonder,
Yonder.

Ribblesdale

Earth, sweet Earth, sweet landscape, with leavès throng
And louchèd low grass, heaven that dost appeal
To, with no tongue to plead, no heart to feel;
That canst but only be, but dost that long –

Thou canst but be, but that thou well dost; strong
Thy plea with him who dealt, nay does now deal,
Thy lovely dale down thus and thus bids reel
Thy river, and o'er gives all to rack or wrong.

    And what is Earth's eye, tongue, or heart else, where
Else, but in dear and dogged man? – Ah, the heir
To his own selfbent so bound, so tied to his turn,
To thriftless reave both our rich round world bare
And none reck of world after, this bids wear
Earth brows of such care, care and dear concern.

Letters

(1879–1883)

To Robert Bridges, May 26, 1879, from Oxford

Dearest Bridges, – Your answerable letterage is three deep at least, but nevertheless work is work and of late Fr. Parkinson has sprung a leak (eczema) in his leg and been laid up and I in consequence laid on all the harder . . .

The sestet of the Purcell sonnet is not so clearly worked out as I cd. wish. The thought is that as the seabird opening his wings with a whiff of wind in your face means the whirr of the motion, but also unaware gives you a whiff of knowledge about his plumage, the marking of which stamps his species, that he does not mean, so Purcell, seemingly intent only on the thought or feeling he is to express or call out, incidentally lets you remark the individualising marks of his own genius.

Sake is a word I find it convenient to use: I did not know when I did so first that it is common in German, in the form *sach*. It is the *sake* of 'for the sake of,' *forsake, namesake, keepsake.* I mean by it the being a thing has outside itself, as a voice by its echo, a face by its reflection, a body by its shadow, a man by his name, fame, or memory, *and also* that in the thing by virtue of which it has especially this being abroad. . . .

Wuthering is a Northcountry word for the noise and rush of wind: hence Emily Brontë's 'Wuthering Heights'.

By *moonmarks* I mean crescent shaped markings on the quill-feathers, either in the colouring of the feather or made by the overlapping of one on another. . . .

To Robert Bridges, October 25, 1879

. . . I think then no one can admire beauty of the body more than I do, and it is of course a comfort to find beauty in a friend or a friend in beauty. But this kind of beauty is dangerous. Then comes the beauty of the mind, such as genius, and this is greater than the beauty of the body and not to call dangerous. And more beautiful than the beauty of the mind is beauty of character. . . .

To Robert Bridges, June 5, 1882, from Roehampton

Dearest Bridges, . . . I have been studying the cuckoo's song. I find it to vary much. In the first place cuckoos do not always sing (or the same cuckoo does not always sing) at the same pitch or in the same key: there are, so to say, alto cuckoos and tenor cuckoos. In particular they sing lower in flying and the interval is then also least, it being an effort to them to strike the higher note, which is therefore more variable than the other. When they perch they sing wrong at first, I mean they correct their first try, rising the upper note. The interval varies as much as a common fourth and this last is the tune when the bird is in loud and good song. . . .

To Robert Bridges, June 10, 1882, from Roehampton

Dearest Bridges, . . . I wish our procession since you were to see it, had been better: I find it is agreed it was heavy and dead. Now a Corpus Christi procession shd. be stately indeed, but it shd. be brisk and joyous. But I grieve more, I am vexed, that you had not a book to follow the words sung: the office is by St. Thomas and contains all his hymns, I think. These hymns, though they have the imperfect rhetoric and weakness in idiom of all Medieval Latin verse (except, say, the *Dies Irae:* I do not mean weakness in classical idiom – that does not matter – but want of feeling). . . .

It is long since such things had any significance for you. But what is strange and unpleasant is that you sometimes speak as if they had in reality none for me and you were only waiting with a certain disgust till I too should be disgusted with myself enough to throw off the mask. You said something of the sort walking on the Cowley Road when we were last at Oxford together – in '79 it must have been. Yet I can hardly think you do not think I am in earnest. And let me say, to take no higher ground, that without earnestness there is nothing sound or beautiful in character and that a cynical vein much indulged coarsens everything in us. Not that you do overindulge this vein in other matters: why then does it bulk out in that diseased and varicose way in this? . . .

To Robert Bridges, June 16, 1882, from Roehampton

Dearest Bridges, – But at any rate do not come on Sunday, for I shall be away taking duty at Westminster.

Put S.W. after Roehampton: your last note had five postmarks, one of them very sinister, as if there had been some struggling or straying.

Corpus Xti differs from all other feasts in this, that its reason and occasion is present. . . . Corpus Christi is the feast of the Real Presence; therefore it is the most purely joyous of solemnities. Naturally the Blessed Sacrament is carried in procession at it, as you saw. But the procession has more meaning and mystery than this: it represents the process of the Incarnation and the world's redemption. As Christ went forth from the bosom of The Father as the Lamb of God and Eucharistic victim to die upon the altar of the cross for the world's ransom; then rising returned leading the procession of the flock redeemed / so in this ceremony his body in *statu victimali* is carried to the Altar of Repose as it is called and back to the tabernacle at the high altar, which will represent the bosom of the godhead. The procession out may represent the cooperation of the angels, or of the patriarchs and prophets, the return the Church Catholic from Christ's death to the end of time. If these things are mismanaged, as they mostly are, it is not for want of significance in the ceremony. . . .

To Robert Bridges, October 18, 1882, from Stonyhurst

Dearest Bridges, – I have read of Whitman's 1) 'Pete' in the library at Bedford Square (and perhaps something else; if so I forget), which you pointed out; 2) two pieces in the *Athenaeum* or *Academy*, one on the Man-of-War Bird, the other beginning 'Spirit that formed this scene'; 3) short extracts in a review by Saintsbury in the *Academy*: this is all I remember. I cannot have read more than half a dozen pieces at most.

This, though very little, is quite enough to give a strong impression of his marked and original manner and way of thought and in particular of his rhythm. . . .

The question then is only about the fact. But first I may as well say what I should not otherwise have said, that I always knew in my heart Walt Whitman's mind to be more like my own than any other man's living. As he is a very great scoundrel this is not a pleasant confession. And this also makes me the more desirous to read him and the more determined that I will not. . . .

To Robert Bridges, January 4, 1883, from Stonyhurst

Dearest Bridges, – Since our holidays began I have been in a wretched state of weakness and weariness, I can't tell why, always drowsy and incapable of reading or thinking to any effect. And this must be why I was, before that, able to do so little on your *Prometheus*. . . .

To return to your sonnet, could you not find another rhyme? there is *spoil, despoil, turmoil,* not to speak of *coil, boil, parboil,* and Hoyle on whist – the very sight of which dreary jugglery brings on yawns with me.

You speak of writing the sonnet in prose first. I read the other day that Virgil wrote the *Aeneid* in prose. Do you often do so? Is it a good plan? If it is I will try it; it may help on my flagging and almost spent powers. Years ago one of ours, a pupil of mine, was to write some English verses for me, to be recited: he had a real vein. He said he had no thoughts, but that if I would furnish some he would versify them. I did so and the effect was very surprising to me to find my own thoughts, with no variation to speak of, expressed in good verses quite unlike mine.

The sonnet on Purcell means this: 1–4. I hope Purcell is not damned for being a Protestant, because I love his genius. 5–8. And that not so much for gifts he shares, even though it shd. be in higher measure, with other musicians as for his own individuality. 9–14. So that while he is aiming only at impressing me his hearer with the meaning in hand I am looking out meanwhile for his specific, his individual markings and mottlings, 'the sakes of him'. It is as when a bird thinking only of soaring spreads its wings: a beholder may happen then to have his attention drawn by the act to the plumage displayed. – In particular, the first lines mean: May Purcell, O may he have died a good death and that soul which I love so much and which breathes or stirs so unmistakeably in his works have parted from the body and passed away, centuries since though I frame the wish, in peace with God! so that the heavy condemnation under which he outwardly or nominally lay for being out of the true Church may in consequence of his good intentions have been reversed. 'Low lays him' is merely 'lays him low', that is / strikes him heavily, weighs upon him. (I daresay this will strike you as more professional than you had anticipated.) It is somewhat dismaying to find I am so unintelligible though, especially in one of my very best pieces. 'Listed', by the by, is 'enlisted'. 'Sakes' is hazardous: about that point I was more bent on saying my say than on being understood in it. The 'moonmarks' belong to the image only of course, not to the application; I mean not detailedly: I was thinking of a bird's quill feathers. One thing disquiets me: *I meant* 'fair fall' to mean *fair (fortune be) fall;* it has since struck me that perhaps 'fair' is an adjective proper and in the predicate and can only be used in cases like 'fair fall the day', that is, *may the day fall, turn out, fair.* My line will yield a sense that way indeed, but I never meant it so. Do you know any passage decisive on this?

Would that I had Purcell's music here. . . .

To Robert Bridges, January 14, 1883, from Stonyhurst

. . . I am here to coach classics for the London University Intermediate (say Moderations) and B.A. (say Greats) examinations. I like my pupils and do not wholly dislike the work, but I fall into or continue in a heavy weary state of body and mind in which my go is gone (the elegance of that phrase! As Thackeray says, it makes one think what vast sums must have been spent on my education!), I make no way with what I read, and seem but half a man. It is a sad thing to say. I try, and am even meant to try, in my spare time (and if I were fresher or if it were anyone but myself there would be a good deal of spare time . . .) to write some books; but I find myself so tired or harassed I fear they will never be written. . . .

To Robert Bridges, February 3, 1883, from Stonyhurst

Dearest Bridges, – I cd. not venture to ask that our library should subscribe half a sovereign for an *édition de luxe* of a new book by an almost unknown author; still less could I expect, nor shd. I like, you to present me, that is our library, with a copy. Here then is a downright deadlock and there is nothing for it. . . .

This is a terrible business about my sonnet 'Have fair fallen', for I find that I still 'make myself misunderstood'. Have is not a plural at all, far from it. It is the singular imperative (or optative if you like) of the past, a thing possible and actual both in logic and grammar, but naturally a rare one. As in the second person we say 'Have done' or in making appointments 'Have had your dinner beforehand', so one can say in the third person not 'Fair fall' of what is present or future but also 'Have fair fallen' of what is past. . . .

This [true virtue] is that chastity of mind which seems to lie at the very heart and be the parent of all other good, the seeing at once what is best, the holding to that, and the not allowing anything else whatever to be even heard pleading to the contrary. Christ's life and character are such as appeal to all the world's admiration, but there is one insight St. Paul gives us of it which is very secret and seems to me more touching and constraining than everything else is: This mind he says, was in Christ Jesus – he means as man; being in the form of God – that is, finding, as in the first instant of his incarnation he did, his human nature informed by the godhead – he thought it nevertheless no snatching-matter for him to be equal with God, but annihilated himself, taking the form of servant; that is, he could not but see what he was, God, but he would see it as if he did not see it, and be it as if he were not and instead of snatching at once at what all the time was his, or was himself, he emptied or exhausted himself so far as that was possible, of godhead and behaved only as God's slave, as his creature, as man, which also he was, and then being in the guise of man humbled himself to death, the death of the cross. It is this holding of himself back, and not snatching at the truest and highest good, the good that was his right, nay his possession from a past eternity in his other nature, his own being and self, which seems to be the root of all his holiness and the imitation of this the root of all moral good in other men. . . .

To R. W. Dixon, June 25, 1883, from Stonyhurst

My Dear Friend, – I am ashamed to think how long I have let you go unanswered: it was bitter winter weather, I remember you said, when you wrote; but the winter was very late this year. It came March 20. . . .

I have little to say. . . .

My time, as I have said before this, is not so closely employed but that someone else in my place might not do a good deal, but I cannot, and I see no grounded prospect of my ever doing much not only in poetry but in anything at all. At times I do feel this sadly and bitterly, but it is God's will and though no change that I can foresee will happen yet perhaps some may that I do not foresee. – I fumble a little at music, at counterpoint, of which in course of time I shall come to know something; for this, like every other study, after some drudgery yields up its secrets, which seem impenetrable at first. If I could get to accompany my own airs I should, so to say, enter into a new kingdom at once, for I have plenty of tunes ready.

Your health is, I hope, good, for when you wrote you were suffering greatly from the cold. We have had drought in Lancashire, a rare thing: now the fine weather is broken up and there is much rain.

In the sonnet enclosed [*Ribblesdale*] 'louchéd' is a coinage of mine and is to mean much the same as *slouched, slouching.* And I mean 'throng' for an adjective as we use it here in Lancashire.

This is but a scrub of a letter, but I could not make it longer or better now.

Believe me your affectionate friend

Gerard M. Hopkins S.J.

To Robert Bridges, July 26, 1883, from Stonyhurst

Dearest Bridges, – . . . Our year begins with autumn and the appointments for this college will be made public on the 1st of next month. It seems likely that I shall be removed; where I have no notion. But I have long been Fortune's football and am blowing up the bladder of resolution big and buxom for another kick of her foot. I shall be sorry to leave Stonyhurst; but go or stay, there is no likelihood of my ever doing anything to last. And I do not know how it is, I have no disease, but I am always tired, always jaded, though work is not heavy, and the impulse to do anything fails me or has in it no continuance.

Weather has been very wet and cold and has made me ill a little.

Believe me your affectionate friend

Gerard

Sermons

After ordination Hopkins's superiors moved him around from parish to parish, looking for the place where he would be most useful. Unfortunately, Hopkins's idiosyncrasies were to get in the way of his connecting with the impoverished parishioners. He tried to make his sermons clear and simple, but often failed to reach his listeners' hearts. Christopher Devlin, editor of a book of Hopkins's sermons, remarks that Hopkins was "wounded three times in his expectation of a full and useful life: first as a scholar, secondly as a preacher, and thirdly as a writer."[31]

It is easy to see how someone as unpredictable as Hopkins might fail to succeed as a preacher. After he used the word "sweetheart" in a sermon, his superior required him to submit notes beforehand so that they could be checked before he delivered each sermon to a congregation. What follows are prepared sermon notes, often unpunctuated and abbreviated.

March 11, 1877

Six months before ordination, Hopkins gave this practice sermon in the refectory at St. Beuno's.

A.M.D.G.[32]

Dixit ergo Jesus: Facite homines discumbere – Then Jesus said:
Make the men sit down (John 6:10).

And now, brethren, you have heard the Gospel of Christ feeding 5000 men with five loaves in the wilderness and how they would have made Him king. Let us do as we are accustomed – return to the story, turn it over and dwell on it, go in mind to that time and in spirit to that place, admire what Christ says as if we heard it, and what He does as if we saw it, until the heart perhaps may swell with pride for Jesus Christ the king of glory. Being a number here together we can do much, we can do what one could not do; I beg of you to lend me your ears and go along with me, in mind, I say, and in spirit, not in the body, for you are as when Our Lord said: make the men sit down; and at the end of all we will crown Christ king – how and where are we to crown Him? In our hearts and souls: he will not make away to the mountain, He wishes for that crowning, He requires it. And in the meanwhile let the men sit down, that is / be at rest, be still, be attentive, listen for what is to come: our Lord by this gospel gives out the living bread of His teaching, I will hand it on to you. . . .

Jesus said to Philip, writes St. John, *where are we to buy bread that these may eat? Where,* said the Word of God, *where,* said the uncreated wisdom speaking to His creature, *shall we buy bread for these to eat? This He said to try him for He Himself knew,* had made up His mind, *what He was going to do. . . .* If St. Philip could not tell himself surely he might have answered: My Lord, Thou Knowest. This would have shewn his faith if not his willingness. But you and I, my brethren, fail much more disgracefully than this apostle did, whose name God glorify. He truly was at his wits' end, he really saw no human way out of that difficulty, he only forgot to think of a miracle; we despair even when humanly the likelihoods are in our favour; if we are sad we think we shall never be happy more, though the same thing has happened to us times and times; if we are sick we despair of being ever well, though nature every day is in some one or other sickening and recovering. . . . Whereas *they that trust in the Lord are as Mount Sion.*

But now (to return to the gospel and Sea of Galilee), up spoke St. Andrew. St. Andrew was St. Philip's friend; he first called him to Christ; he was always helpful to him; when the Greeks asked to see our Lord timid Philip told Andrew first and *Andrew and Philip* – so the Scripture says – told Jesus. St. Andrew took one step, it was but a little one but he took it: he went and found out what food there was to be had – it was five loaves and two fishes. . . . Here then he put in a helpful word: *There is a boy here has five barley loaves and two fishes, but* – . . . *a little boy* it is in the Greek, *just a boy* in the Latin: certainly a little boy, just a boy, could not carry much: the beginning is bad enough. The continuance is worse: who has five barley loaves and two fishes: to be sure a little boy, just a boy, might carry that much well enough. Five barley loaves, not quartern loaves but what they call breads abroad, more like rolls than loaves, and five in number: if one could make a man's dinner then five of the apostles might have dined and the rest of the apostles and all the disciples and all the multitude gone without. . . .

But God asks but very little of His creatures; sometimes to be willing, just to shew they are willing, is enough, and He will do the rest. Our Lord had got from one of His disciples a weak but helping hand, one wavering suggestion and He was satisfied. The lord and master spoke now: *Make the men sit down.* In the meantime the bread and the fish were sent for and laid before Him. Undoubtedly the hearts of the disciples were beating with awe and expectation at what was next to come. And at the same time the gentle but great and undeniable word was in their ears driving them down into the thousands below: *Make those men sit down.* They had not thought of asking Him to share His power, dull, disrespectful, faithless that they had been, they had complained of His teaching too long, of having to go far to get bread, of two hundred pennyworth not being enough, of five loaves being lost among so many; their master had seemed to notice nothing, to let things go too far, to need their advice, to want their help. Suddenly the thunder had rolled over their heads, harmless but unmistakable the tongue of the heavenly lightning had rushed downwards before their eyes, and all the place was full of the sense of royal majesty, of more than prophetic power, of divine glory: *Make the men sit down.* All was ready, there was much soft green grass in the place. Down fell the men to table – the table was the grass – not so much with eagerness for the meal as with awe and necessity at the command, five thousand in number. Not that it was done in a moment, but it was done with royal, with military strength, hearing of no denial. The twelve apostles, the many disciples went forth; they stemmed their way through the throng; they gave the word, You here, you there; fifty in this company, a hundred in that; not one man more, not one less; down I tell you, the master has spoken. The crowd forestalled the command, in joyous fear down they fell; they broke into plots and lots, they parted into platoons and square companies; the fifty-one sent off their fifty-first man, they dared not keep him; the forty-nine beckoned him, he must come. The master had spoken: *Make the men sit down.* . . . 5000 grown men like chidden children crouched to the ground at the word which made the men sit down.

And now, brethren, think you see them like a well drilled army encamped on the green field, think you see the joyous green grass of that spring plotted with flowerbeds of human limbs and faces. The thunderclap has spoken and passed: Make the men sit down / and the rain of the gracious and divine providential mercy has set in. As when a sheet of white rain coming from the sea blots out first the Orms' Heads on Moel Hiraddug, then spreads mile after mile, from hill to hill, from square to square of the fields, along the Vale of Clwyd, so the refreshment of the barley bread was spreading through that multitude. The apostles and disciples went and came, setting out with loaded baskets, returning with empty ones; the whole scene was in circulation, the flow of food unbroken; the awestruck and astonished crowd look now this way, now that, they see our Lord higher up on the hillside with a little parcel of something eatable before Him, dealing and dealing and dealing it out; it works its way in streams of disciples, it spreads inexhaustibly over the face of the multitude. . . . As the yeast pushes and blisters up in the dark kneading trough: so this in open daylight and yet no one can exactly see when and how, grows under the very hands that deal it. . . . And so they receive each his piece of barley bread and of the fish as much as they want, all eat and are filled and the remainder fills twelve baskets.

Much, much more might be said, for the meaning of the Scripture, like this very bread, grows and multiplies as you deal it out. But we will leave the multitude there, orderly strewn on the fresh green grass, enjoying the heavenly festival under Christ's eyes, then rising with untaught mistaken zeal to make Him king. . . .

How was this sermon received? Hopkins himself reports: "People laughed at it prodigiously, I saw some of them roll on their chairs with laughter. This made me lose the thread, so that I did not deliver the last two paragraphs right but mixed things up. The last paragraph, in which 'Make the men sit down' is often repeated, far from having a good effect, made them roll more than ever."

OXFORD SERMONS

Hopkins's superiors hoped that he might find his place as a preacher and pastor at Oxford. Since he had gone to school there, he could reach out to students interested in Catholicism without giving offense to the university. In the end, however, he was there only from July to September 1879.

For Sunday, July 6, 1879, Feast of the Precious Blood–to be preached at St. Clement's, Oxford

1. Why it is called Precious;
2. Why it is so precious, so dear, to the Eternal Father;
3. Why it should be so to us
    a. Preciousness of blood in general,
    b. of Christ's in particular

The Scripture says *the blood is the life. It is,* that is to say, *the stream which carries life* round the whole body; when its circulation weakens life lags, when it stops life ceases. Life is precious, it is in this world our being; therefore the blood. . . . It sympathises with life, which is so precious, and so it is precious itself.

We naturally take it as precious. When children see a drop of it spilt, even without pain, they turn pale or shed tears or faint. Many people faint at the sight of much of it. It shews they see in it some great loss, something approaching the loss of life.

Men bring it into their oaths, quite senselessly. But it makes the things they talk of seem important, more worth your listening about than if they did not call them by its name.

Men sign in their own blood to give importance to what is written. . . .

If all blood precious *much more Christ's.* His life the most precious, therefore his blood. *In the natural order* Christ's the most precious body and soul, life, blood. This blood traced from Adam's veins through Abraham's, royal David's, to Mary's; from her blood he took it with all his human frame: it had the *noblest lineage in the world. Beauty and perfection of his body,* its health untouched by any sickness or ache; hence the peerless healthfulness of his blood's beating.

It beat and sympathised with the feelings of his heart, performing nobler offices than any other blood can ever do.

Moreover it was shed, first in small quantity and with comparatively slight pain in the Circumcision; then by dreadful and unnatural channels in the Agony; then cruelly in the scourging, crowning and crucifixion; then so completely after death as to empty the veins. If generous shedding can make blood precious none could be more generously than Christ's. . . .

But *supernaturally* it is far more precious. It is *united to the Word of God,* who was made flesh and therefore blood, for flesh is not without blood. It is, every drop of it is, as holy as God himself. No wonder then it is called precious. . . .

(Here ought be added that it was precious, that is / that it must be precious, because of what it purchased, the whole world) . . .

It is so especially precious and *dear to the Eternal Father because it is the blood of the great sacrifice,* not only his divine son's blood but that shed in his honour, shed as an act of perfect devotion of the utmost piety towards him.

Religion is the highest of the moral virtues and sacrifice the highest act of religion. Also self sacrifice is the purest charity. Christ was the most religious of men, to offer sacrifice was the chief purpose of his life and that the sacrifice of himself.

For Sunday, August 17, 1879 at St. Clement's

Cure of the Deaf and Dumb Man; *Ephphatha* (Mark 7:31–37).

If we learn no more from a Gospel or a sermon on the Gospel than to know our Lord Jesus Christ better, to be prouder of him, and to love him more we learn enough and we learn a precious lesson. He is the king to whom we are to be loyal and he is the general we are to obey. The man that says to himself as he walks: Christ is my king, Christ is my hero, I am at Christ's orders, I am his to command / that man is a child of light – *qui sequitur me non ambulat in tenebris, sed habebit lumen vitae* [33] who follows, etc. So that it would be a good practice if you are walking alone sometimes to say over many times to yourselves: Christ is my master; then after a time: Lord, what wilt thou have me do? Then to answer yourselves: My daily duties, just the duties of my station / and: I wish to do my daily duties to thy glory, my God / and in particular you may name one or more. This is mental prayer.

After saying this need only point out how our Lord behaved in the case before us. *He behaved with gentleness and secrecy* according to his wisdom; at other times according to the same wisdom with sternness and open vehemence, but here with gentleness and secrecy.

They bring him *a deaf and dumb man to be cured.* We learn from St. Matthew that *he had a devil.* That is / his deafness and etc., were not natural nor due to faults of the organs, an evil spirit had possessed himself of them; a sullen, stubborn spirit, hiding both himself and his victim's reason. Therefore not generally known that he was possessed, this dreadful circumstance could be concealed, and the evangelist conceals it because Christ did so. It is true we learn it from St. Matthew, but after a time all reason for concealment passed away, the people could no longer be identified. To conceal then this painful circumstance our Lord took the sufferer aside. Here you see his considerateness for his creatures' feelings.

He put his fingers into the man's ears – as if to break down the hindrance which barred up his hearing and deafened him; but gently, with the fingertips, as if it were some delicate operation the heavenly physician had in hand, not a work of mighty power. Those things which are said to be done by the Lord's arm are God's works of power; those by his finger are the subtle workings of his wisdom. Here we may understand how men through sin had become deaf to God's calls, when his son, coming in flesh, by his gentle dealings with them once more opened their hearts.

He touched his tongue with spittle from his mouth. When the mouth is parched and dry it is hard to speak, moistening it gives it the power of speech again. Here we may understand how men had ceased to pray, or to pray as they should. . . . When Christ by the sweetness of the lessons of his mouth made their tongues free and lissome again.

Then having made the organs ready to hear and speak *he looked up to heaven and groaned* – It was an appeal, a prayer to his heavenly Father, full of pity for this poor possessed man and for all mankind. *And he said: Ephphatha, Be opened* – The evangelist tells us the very word which had this magical or rather miraculous effect. He spoke to the man and not rebuked the devil, but the devil nevertheless fled away, *And immediately, etc.*

Then our Lord told the cured patient and his friends *not to speak of it,* but the ears he had opened did not heed him nor the tongue he had loosened obey. Nevertheless little harm, as I suppose, was done by this: for their own interest he had kept the matter quiet and bidden them do so; but, if they chose to speak their interests and their good name were now in their own keeping to do as they liked with. Besides he would not punish them for preferring his honour to their own.

He hath done all things well, etc. – that is / the whole thing. They admired the completeness and delicacy of the cure. Much more should we admire what Christ has done for us – made us deaf hear, if we will hear, not with a touch of his fingertips but with his hands hardnailed out and appealingly stretched on the cross; made us dumb speak in praise and prayer to God not by a moistening of spittle but by the shedding of his precious blood.

For Sunday, September 7, 1879 at St. Aloysius, Oxford

Gospel from the Sermon on the Mount, *No man can serve two masters,* etc., (Matt. 6:24–34).

You cannot serve God and Mammon – Who is this Mammon that is God's rival? Mammon means Treasure or Riches: some say he was the god of riches among the Syrians, as Plutus among the Greeks. But no mention of him is made by ancient writers. Why then are Riches spoken of as if some person? Why say Mammon as if it were someone's name? – To answer this, watch some man who 'hastens to be rich', goes to work early, works hard, returns late, spares his purse, scants his pleasures, and ask for whose sake he lives thus, *slaves* thus? Not for God's, he does not pretend it; nor for his own, for he seeks his peace neither in the world to come nor yet in this; then surely for some hard master, behind the scenes; but no, we know there is no such personage, money is his master and money is no person; therefore our Lord gives it a name as if it were some person, some idol, some god, being only money all the while.

We cannot then serve God and do what he asks of us if our first thought is of money or other worldly goods. But yet we must take some thought of them and the question is how much. For no one is to be idle and shelter his sluggishness behind this text, since St. Paul plainly says / If a man will not work neither shall he eat. Then how much? This is an important question and must be answered with heed and care. . . .

To the question then / How much care we may take of money and worldly goods / we have Christ's answer / Seek first, etc. That is where God's service and the world's clash. God is the master, not the world, God must be obeyed, the world neglected. In other words he who would keep God's commandments but aims at nothing higher may take as much care of money as will not make him break the commandments and fall into mortal sin. But for one who wishes to keep Christ's counsels the answer is / Provide for necessities and leave the rest to God and to such a man this Gospel comes most home.

Do not be anxious, he says, and he gives a reason full of wisdom. Is not the life more? etc., This might seem a reason for being anxious, for the life must be kept up by food, the body protected by clothing. Only the food is for the life, not the life for the food; the clothing for etc. When therefore we have necessary food and clothing we have enough: Having food and clothing, the Apostle says, let us be content. The life is more than the food; it is against reason, it is the cart before the horse to wear out life in toiling for food; to waste and weary the body in labouring for clothing. By food and clothing understand all things that support and furnish us in our way of life.

Bedford Leigh was a grimy, poverty-stricken industrial town near Manchester. Sent there for three months because no one else was available, Hopkins found a place where his erudition was useless, but his physical presence was appreciated. Devlin writes, "It was then and there, during that stop-gap period and in that incongruous place, that he found the greatest happiness in his pastoral life and the most fruitful work. . . . In this smoke-sodden little town he came up against people who needed him desperately, and their need was what he needed."[34]

For Sunday, October 5, 18th after Pentecost at St. Joseph's, Bedford Leigh

The Cure of the Sick of the Palsy (Matt. 9:1–8, see also Mark 2:3 sqq., Luke 5:18 sqq.).

They brought to him one sick of the palsy – let us consider the affliction of this man and of all sufferers from palsy or paralysis. Palsy is the most thorough of all cripplings, it is a living death. The poor and wretched, the hungry, the unhappy can stir abroad; prisoners can move in their cells though small and help themselves; the sick can hope for recovery and then to go about; the bedridden even can stir their limbs and feel some power in them; but to the palsied not only their bedroom is their tomb, their bed their coffin, their linen their shroud, but their very body is their corpse, and yet they live. Despair of relief, helplessness, shame at being thrown on others, all afflict the palsied man.

Nevertheless all is not lost, they might well be worse – for *they have power of the mind*, that is not palsied that works and has its play. That has neither the feebleness of childhood nor the dotage of age nor the ravings of fever nor the foul mouth of drunkenness, nor the driveling of idiocy nor the frenzy of madness. They can help themselves by speech or, if that too is gone, still by some sign and get others to do for them what they cannot do themselves. See what spirits and energy this man had. He did not call our Lord to him or meet him in the way or come to him in quiet or even push his way where he was through the crowd; nothing would do but if he could be got at no way else he would break an entrance through a roof and be swung down in his bed. For so we read in the two other accounts. The place described. Imagine then the surprise of those assembled there, the sound of feet scrambling on the tiles, the light of heaven breaking in, a mattress coming through swung by four ends of rope, and a man that had for many years perhaps been confined to one room now dangling between heaven and earth over the heads of a crowd of strangers.

Thy sins are forgiven thee – All were wondering what Christ would say and do. He began by forgiving sin. Now this had not been asked. The sick man perhaps felt a pang of disappointment. It is so hard to set the soul above the body, our spiritual good and interests above our temporal. And the scribes blasphemed. But let us consider the wisdom of our Lord's behavior:

This sick man and his bearers had come to him to get from him some good, and a crowd had followed and was round him. A crowd had followed him: they followed him in the wilderness heedless of food; they so came and went that we read the disciples had not time to get a meal; here they so crowded him that the bearers had not been able to come through. And the more the crowd made it hard to come at him the more they were bent on doing it, for the harder the work the more it seemed worth doing. But what does a crowd prove? Any quack or false prophet, any conjuror or showman can draw a crowd. Now mark these two classes of people. The quack and false prophet offer something worth having – the health of the body or the knowledge of God; but they are impostors and lie, and what they offer they cannot give. On the other hand the conjuror and showman are honest, they can display something out of the common and that others cannot do, but then the things they show are little worth. Now the crowd might go to our Lord as to a show out of curiosity, which is no virtuous motive; or for their soul's good, as to a prophet, which is a virtuous motive; or as to a physician, for their body's good which is betwixt and between. As to a show, for he worked miracles, which are more worth witnessing than any conjuring: the one is the sleight of hand of man, the other is the finger of God. And we know they did come to our Lord not to hear him but to have their fill of bread brought to them by a miracle. Christ could not then be satisfied that men should come to him as to one who could shew them a sight of miracles, as though he were no more than a divine conjuror come down from heaven for their idle wonder. This was what Herod wanted him to be. Nor could he be satisfied if they came to him as a physician, for so they might to any physician that could cure them, not come from heaven, and their souls be no better after the cure. Or they might come to him as a prophet: but then there are false prophets and no more could he be satisfied that they should come to him with the same disposition as with no better proof that he came from God than if it were an impostor in God's name that they went to. He had then to do two things – to set their dispositions right, making them look to what was holy and spiritual, not what was low and temporal, and again to guide their faith, that it might rest on God's word and not on man's. There were the scribes also to be set right. When they heard him say / Thy sins, etc. they had said he blasphemed. They meant that being man he took to himself power that belonged only to God. And they blasphemed themselves. Consider how rash and wrong these bad men were. For either Christ was God as well as man, or he was man only and neither way would he blaspheme. If God, etc., he could forgive sins. If man only, still God could give him power to forgive sins as he gives it to priests now. But they blasphemed both God's person and his power – his person, the second person of the Trinity there before them, and his power denying that he could give power to man. He had then to lift up the thoughts of those who came to him to the things of God and, that done, to rebuke the unfaith of some and confirm the faith of others by a mark that God had sent him. With this, brethren, now mark the wisdom and subtlety of what he did.

He begins by raising their minds to the true and best good, the soul's good: thy sins, he said to the man, are forgiven thee. Then he leads them to the faith of God. *Whither is easier?* he asks. Mark this: he does not say / which is easier to *do*? For we know it is easier to heal the body than the soul. But his question is / which is easier to *say?* which costs the speaker most? For / Thy sins are forgiven thee, any impostor can say that. Who will know? The soul is not seen; sick or sound, disfigured with sin or lovely with grace, it does not come before men's eyes; and if you profess to heal it and do not, who is the wiser? But say to a cripple / Arise and walk, and the next minute shews whether you have power from God or no. If then Christ could in the power of God say the harder / Arise and walk / and what he said be done: so in the power of God he could say the less hard / Thy sins are forgiven thee / and what he said be done there too. *Then said he to the sick of the palsy* etc. Fancy the shudder of fear and the leap of joy that passed through them when they saw that man could not lift of himself one trembling limb – rise hale and strong, shoulder the mattress that had so long carried him, and thrust his way through the home. . . .

For Sunday, November 16, 24th after Pentecost, Gospel from 6th after Epiphany

The Mustard Seed and the Leaven (Matt. 13:31–35, see also Mark 4:30 sqq., Luke 13:18 sqq.).

Christ compares the Kingdom of Heaven, that is his Church, to this and to that; the Kingdom of Heaven, he says, is like . . . ; but *it cannot be said he compares it to what is all good.* He clearly shews, and he takes pains to shew, it will be mingled, that is in this world it will, of many sorts, of good, bad, and indifferent. (Here quote the Ten Virgins and the Net.) And yet men are scandalised when they find it not all perfect: here there is one bad, there a bad family, somewhere else, a bad town or country, and one whole age of the Church may be not so good as another. There will be black sheep among the white; there will be even bad shepherds, I mean priests, the pastors of Christ's flock. Scandals must come, only woe to him, etc.

In the place this Gospel is taken from Christ speaks of the Kingdom of Heaven in four or five parables (see St. Mark for one, 4:26.), there may have been more. The first is that of the Sower: this rings out that the good seed may fail for want of good ground. Another is that of the Cockle: this shews that it may be mingled with evil seed when there is an evil sower. But to shew the fault is not in what God gives but in the way it is dealt with he tells three other parables, one how the corn grows though the farmer takes no notice of it (Mark); the second of the mustard seed; the third of the leaven. The Mustard Seed shews the Kingdom of Heaven has in it a prodigious life and power of growing; the Leaven shews its power to act upon the world.

To compare God's kingdom to a mustard plant seems quaint and odd. We read that our Lord said / What is the kingdom of Heaven like and to what shall I liken it? as though he himself were astonished at it and could in all his world find nothing that could be its match. Then he found the mustard plant. He meant not our mustard plant, which does not grow high, but the tall mustard of the East: it grows so high that it is not a herb at all nor even a bush but a tree outright. What he says of the seed must be taken roughly, that it is very small; for no doubt there are others smaller, even that cannot be seen with the naked eye.

But why is the Kingdom of Heaven like this plant? – Because its beginnings are very small and it grows to very great. . . .

For Sunday Evening, November 23, 1879

And the child's father and mother were amazed at what was being said about him (Luke 2:33).

St. Joseph though he often carried our Lord Jesus Christ in his arms and the Blessed Virgin though she gave him birth and suckled him at her breast, though they seldom either of them had the holy child out of their sight and knew more of him far than all others, yet when they heard what Holy Simeon a stranger had to say of him the Scripture says they wondered. Not indeed that they were surprised and had thought to hear something different but that they gave their minds up to admiration and dwelt with reverent wonder on all God's doings about the child their sacred charge. Brethren, see what a thing it is to hear about our Lord Jesus Christ, to think of him and dwell upon him; it did good to those two holiest people the Blessed Virgin and St. Joseph, even with him in the house God thought fit to give them lights by the mouth of strangers. It cannot but do good to us, who have more need of holiness, who easily forget Christ, who have not got him before our eyes to look at. . . .

I come to his mind. He was the greatest genius that ever lived. You know what genius is, brethren – beauty and perfection in the mind. . . . You must not say, Christ needed no such thing as genius; his wisdom came from heaven, for he was God. To say so is to speak like the heretic Apollinaris, who said that Christ had indeed a human body but no soul, he needed no mind and soul, for his godhead, the Word of God, that stood for mind and soul in him. No, but Christ was perfect man and must have mind as well as body and that mind was, no question, of the rarest excellence and beauty; it was genius. As Christ lived and breathed and moved in a true and not a phantom human body and in that laboured, suffered, was crucified, died, and was buried; as he merited by acts of his human will; so he reasoned and planned and invented by acts of his own human genius, genius made perfect by wisdom of its own, not the divine wisdom only.

A witness to his genius we have in those men who being sent to arrest him came back empty handed, spellbound by his eloquence, saying / Never man spoke like this man.

A better proof we have in his own words, his Sermon on the Mount, his parables, and all his sayings recorded in the Gospel. My brethren, we are so accustomed to them that they do not strike us as they do a stranger that hears them first, else we too should say / Never man, etc. No stories or parables are like Christ's, so bright, so pithy, so touching; no proverbs or sayings are such jewellery: they stand off from other men's thoughts like stars, like lilies in the sun; nowhere in literature is there anything to match the Sermon on the Mount: if there is let men bring it forward. Time does not allow me to call your minds to proofs or instances. Besides Christ's sayings in the Gospels a dozen or so more have been kept by tradition and are to be found in the works of the Fathers and early writers and one even in the Scripture itself: It is more blessed, etc. When these sayings are gathered together, though one cannot feel sure of every one, yet reading all in one view they make me say / These must be Christ's, never man, etc. One is: Never rejoice but when you look upon your brother in love. Another is: My mystery is for me and for the children of my house. . . .

Now in the third place, far higher than beauty of the body, higher than genius and wisdom the beauty of the mind, comes the beauty of his character, his character as man. For the most part his very enemies, those that do not believe in him, allow that a character so noble was never seen in human mould. Plato the heathen, the greatest of the Greek philosophers, foretold of him; he drew by his wisdom a picture of the just man in his justice crucified and it was fulfilled in Christ. Poor was his station, laborious his life, bitter his ending: through poverty, through labour, through crucifixion his majesty of nature more shines. No heart as his was ever so tender, but tenderness was not all: this heart so tender was as brave, it could be stern. He found the thought of his Passion past bearing, yet he went through with it. He was feared when he chose: he took a whip and singlehanded cleared the temple. The thought of his gentleness towards children, towards the afflicted, towards sinners, is often dwelt on; that of his courage less. But for my part I like to feel that I should have feared him. We hear also of his love, as for John and Lazarus; and even love at first sight, as of the young man that had kept all the commandments from his childhood. But he warned or rebuked his best friends when need was, as Peter, Martha, and even his mother. For, as St. John says, he was full both of grace and of truth.

But, brethren, from all that might be said of his character I single out one point and beg you to notice that. He loved to praise, he loved to reward. He knew what was in man, he best knew men's faults and yet he was the warmest in their praise. When he worked a miracle he would grace it with / Thy faith hath saved thee, that it might almost seem the receiver's work, not his. He said of Nathanael that he was an Israelite without guile; he that searches hearts said this, and yet what praise that was to give! He called the two sons of Zebedee Sons of Thunder, kind and stately and honourable name! We read of nothing thunderlike that they did except, what was sinful, to wish fire down from heaven on some sinners, but they deserved the name or he would not have given it, and he has given it them for all time. Of John the Baptist he said that his greater was not born of women. He said to Peter / Thou art Rock / and rewarded a moment's acknowledgement of him with the lasting headship of his Church. He defended Magdalen and took means that the story of her generosity should be told forever. And though he bids *us* say we are unprofitable servants, yet he himself will say to each of us / Good and faithful servant, well done.

And this man whose picture I have tried to draw for you, brethren, is your God. He was your maker in time past; hereafter he will be your judge. Make him your hero now. Take some time to think of him; praise him in your hearts. You can over your work or on your road, praise him, saying over and over again / Glory be to Christ's body; Glory to the body of the Word made flesh; Glory to the body suckled at the Blessed Virgin's breasts; Glory to Christ's body in its beauty; Glory to Christ's body in its weariness; Glory to Christ's body in its Passion, death and burial; Glory to Christ's body risen; Glory to Christ's body in the Blessed Sacrament; Glory to Christ's soul; Glory to his genius and wisdom; Glory to his unsearchable thoughts; Glory to his saving words; Glory to his sacred heart; Glory to its courage and manliness; Glory to its meekness and mercy; Glory to its every heartbeat, to its joys and sorrows, wishes, fears; Glory in all things to Jesus Christ God and man. If you try this when you can you will find your heart kindle and while you praise he will praise you – a blessing, etc.

For Sunday Morning, November 30, 1879, First of Advent, at St. Joseph's, Bedford

If the Spirit of him who raised Jesus from the dead dwells in you, he who raised Christ from the dead will give life to your mortal bodies also through his Spirit that dwells in you.

So then, brothers and sisters, we are debtors, not to the flesh, to live according to the flesh – for if you live according to the flesh, you will die; but if by the Spirit you put to death the deeds of the body, you will live. For all who are led by the Spirit of God are children of God (Rom. 8:11–14).

. . . Now, Brethren, as the time of Christ's second coming is uncertain so is the time of our death. Both are certain to come, both are uncertain when. But one thing may be said of both and the apostle says it: The night has got on, the day is nearer. This is, my brethren, always true and always getting truer. Mark these two things: every minute true, for it is at any minute true to say our life has got some way on, our death made some approach, or again that the world has gone on some time since Christ's first coming and made some approach to his second; and also every minute truer for every minute we and the world are older every minute our death and the world's end are nearer than before. For life and time are always losing, always spending, always running down and running out therefore every hour that strikes is a warning of our end and the world's end for both these things are an hour nearer than before. But there is a difference between our death and the world's end: the world's end though every generation, one after another is warned of it, yet one only will be overtaken by it, the rest will have passed away before; but death comes to every one and none escapes. Therefore God has given us more warnings of death: age is a warning, sickness is a warning, and the deaths of others that go before us are a great warning. For the last day none have seen, but almost all men have seen death.

However, whether for the world's end or death, the apostle's warning is the same, to walk honestly, that is honourably, becomingly, wellbehavedly, as in the day, not etc. And Christ's warning is like it (Luke 21:34): *But take heed to yourselves that your hearts be not loaded with overeating and drunkenness and cares of this life, and that day come upon you unawares.* And these things that they warn us of, they abound; who needs the warning more than we? For the evils abound. Now more than ever is there riotous company, drunkenness, lewdness, strife, brawling, even bloodshed. To speak against all these things is too much. But look, brethren, at the order of them. First comes rioting or revelry, unruly company: here is the beginning of evil, bad company. Bad company seem hearty friends, goodnatured companions and such as a man should have: must not a man have his friend, his companion, unbend from his work at times, see company and life? Must he sit mum? Must he mope at home? But, brethren look at these things nearer. A friend is a friend, he loves you, he thinks of you and not only of his own pleasure. A rout of drinking companions do not love one another, they are selfish, they do not love their own, how can you think they care for strangers? Their own children may be hungry, their mothers or their wives in tears, their homes desolate and they are so good as to spend their time, their money, and their health with you.

One of two things: you treat them or they you. If you treat them you like a fool spend your money on the worthless; if they treat you often you are eating their children's bread, you are draining the blood of their little ones. There is no friendship here, no love; there is no love, I say, where nothing comes in but selfishness.

And unruly company leads to drunkenness. Though many and many a tongue is not telling of it what tongue *can* tell the evils of drunkenness? – Drunkenness is shameful, it makes the man a beast; it drowns noble reason, their eyes swim, they hiccup in their talk, they gabble and blur their words, they stagger and fall and deal themselves dishonourable wounds, their faces grow blotched and bloated, scorpions are in their mind, they see devils and frightful sights. A little drunkenness is sad, a thing pitiful to see, and drunkenness confirmed and incurable is a world of woe. It defiles and dishonours the fresh blooming roses of youth, the strength of manhood, the grey hairs of age. It corrupts the children yet unborn, it gives convulsions to the poor sucking child. It is ugly in man, but in woman it is hideous beyond what words can say. And the world is laid waste with it.

It lays waste a home. There is no peace; there is no reverence or honour. The children are scandalised and taught to sin. Nay, it breaks home quite up, breaks the bond that God fastens, what he has joined it puts asunder, wife runs from drunken husband or husband from drunken wife.

It wastes, it spends, it brings on poverty. Times may be good, wages may abound, and yet in the house is seen want and slovenly disorder, for gold and silver and clothes and furniture and all are gone one way, down the belly. Or times may be bad and then surely there is nothing to spend on drink. But there is: feet may go bare and the hearth be cold but the fire in the throat must be quenched with liquor or rather with liquor fanned to flame.

And not only must the body want the soul too is to fast and lose its food; the family cannot go to mass, obey the Church's commandment, worship God on his holy day in his holy place and be present at the great sacrifice; though it should cost not a penny they cannot do it, because the clothes are pawned.

And lastly drunkenness leads to worse sin than itself, leads to crimes – to cursing, blasphemy, abuse, the foul mouth; to all incontinence and impurity; to brawls and blows and bloodshed.

What then is the remedy? – I am not now, brethren, to speak of rioting and drunkenness in particular, their cause and cure but on the epistle of the day. The cure the Apostle gives is / to put on Jesus Christ, that is the white robe of justice and God's grace or, as he says above, the armour of light. This is a robe, this is armour, that all of you either have never lost or at least can easily put on: You can go to the sacrament of penance. And though temptation is here, because it everywhere abounds, yet this is a place, brethren, where those who will be good can be. Here the young woman can grow up, live, and die in maidenly or in motherly innocence; here the young man can make and keep his strength and manhood sacred to God. And if you have fallen, if you have fouled your white robe and stained your lightsome armour, you can with ease recover all again. God's grace either always to have kept, or having lost, to recover, is a blessing I wish you all.

For Friday Evening, December 5, 1879 at St. Joseph's, Bedford

. . . A king looking among his subjects for a bride to share his throne might say of many a young woman: I could indeed raise so-and-so to be my queen; but she is unworthy, her lowbred manners would soon break out and disgrace the lofty station she was never born to: at last he might find one of whom he could say: Here is maiden that now thinks of no such honour but if I raise her to it she will make it seem that she was born to nothing else, so well will it become her: here is the maiden for me, she and no other shall share my royalty. It was thus God foresaw of the Virgin Mary and predestined her first to be conceived without spot and then to be the mother of his son.

What then were the great virtues he saw in her and so pleased him, which we too may see in her and please him by copying? – I suppose the two virtues she is most famous for are her purity and her humility.

How beautiful is purity! All admire it, at least in others. The most wicked profligate man would wish his mother to have been pure, his wife, sisters, daughters to be pure. And in men it is honoured as in women: the man that this same profligate knows he can trust where he could not himself be trusted he cannot but deeply honour. When purity is lost comes shame and a stain within the mind which, even after God has long forgiven us, it seems our own tears would never wash away. And for this virtue the Blessed Virgin became the mother of God and St. John the bosom friend of the Sacred Heart.

(Some words on humility, which I had not time to write.)

LIVERPOOL SERMONS

In January 1880 Hopkins started preaching at St. Francis Xavier's Church in Liverpool, among Irish immigrant families. He would stay at this post for almost two years. It was not long before his health broke down, and along with the physical malaise rose a mounting sense of his own inadequacy to meet the needs of parishioners living in dire poverty and moral degradation.

For St. Francis Xavier's, Liverpool, Sunday Evening, January 4, 1880

Thy will be done on earth as it is in heaven, taken at random (Matt. 6:10).

A.M.D.G.

We are all of us bound to love God, so bound that if we do not it will be a mortal sin and we shall be lost. For this is God's first and great commandment: *Thou shalt love the Lord thy God with thy whole heart and with thy whole soul and with thy whole mind and with thy whole strength: this is the first commandment* (Mark 12:30). . . .

The love of God *or divine charity is to wish God's will done* and when God's will is against ours to wish his will done rather than ours because God is God and we are only men: this is divine charity, this is to love God, this is to keep the great commandment and all the commandments, this is to be in the way of salvation. He that says, and means, 'Thy will be done on earth as it is in heaven' will in that state of mind be saved, he cannot be lost. I do not care how cold his love may be, he loves God; he may never have shed a tear over Christ's passion, heaved a sigh for his own sins, felt his heart kindle at anything holy, he loves God: he may seem to obey unwillingly, but if he can say / God is God and I am only a man and therefore his will ought to be done in this matter and I will do it / that man loves God and loves God more than himself, that man has divine charity. . . .

In what does love consist? In what is love seen? By what is love tried? – By doing the beloved's will. . . .

Nay, my brethren, *this is not only love but it is as high as the highest.* There is a sweeter, tenderer love, a love more working and effectual, which may be added to it and grow out of it, of that

I shall not speak tonight, but the love I have spoken of comes first and none can be higher. For the love a sovereign first of all and above all claims is the love of him as sovereign: he will be glad of a dearer love than that but he will not insist on it, the doing his sovereign will he will insist on. Say he is popular because he is young and handsome, accomplished, renowned in arms, gracious in his manners, but so may his nobles be or any of his subjects; but there is one love none but he can claim and without that all other love is worthless – obedience. And so with God; gifts will not do nor sacrifices, sighs and tears will not do nor cries of enthusiasm unless his sovereign will is done: obedience is better than sacrifice; seas of tears and sighs to fill the firmament are waste of water and loss of breath where duty is not done. *Duty is love.* What a shame to set duty off against love and bloat ourselves because we act from love and so-and-so, our dull neighbor can but plod his round of duty! *There is nothing higher than duty* in creatures or in God: God the Son's love for God the Father is duty. Only when I speak this highly of duty I mean duty done because it *is* duty and not mainly done from either hope or fear.

Such then my brethren, is love of God, to wish his will done on earth as it is in heaven, their duties done by men as their duties are done by angels, and not wish it done only, but do it; for wishing without doing, where we can do, is not true wishing even. May God's will be done on earth as it is in heaven, a blessing I wish the earth and you in the name, etc.

For Sunday Evening, January 18, 1880, 2nd after Epiphany, at St. Francis Xavier's, Liverpool

God's Kingdom in the Earthly Paradise (text: *Thy kingdom come,* as last Sunday)

Let me recall to your minds, my brethren, *what I said in this place Sunday.* I spoke of God's kingdom, of what is meant by the words, so common in the Gospel, *the Kingdom of God,* that is a sacred commonwealth to which both God belongs and man, God being the sovereign there and men the subjects. For of every commonwealth this is the essence and the nature: it is the meeting of many for their joint and common good, for which good all are solemnly engaged to strive and being so engaged are then in duty bound to strive, the ruler by planning, the ruled by performing, the sovereign by the weight of his author-ity, the subject by the stress of his obedience. This, I say, is what a commonwealth means and God's first kingdom upon earth was such: God had a place in it and man, God was to gain by it and man, God bound himself by duty in it and man, God was justified in it and man. . . . Now then what are the terms of that contract between God and man, in other words what was the constitution of that commonwealth? What was the good it aimed at? What the duties to be done in it? what its laws? and what its forfeits? . . .

Now *what was the common weal?* What was the joint and common good of that kingdom? – it was that God should be glorified in man and man glorified in God. Man was created to praise, honour, and serve God, thus fulfilling God's desire in bringing him into being, and by so doing to save his soul, thus fulfilling his own desire, the desire of everything that has being. He was created to give God glory and by so doing to win himself glory. This was the good that first commonwealth aimed at, this was its common weal; and surely it was the good of all persons, parties, and estates in the commonwealth all bound up together, in a way and to a degree truly worthy of the divine wisdom that planned it.

But *the common good is to be realised,* it is to be brought about, *by all* the citizens or members and estates of the commonwealth *doing their duty:* so we said. A commonwealth, we said, was bound together by duty; the sovereign was bound by duty as the subject. Here then what was the duty God undertook? – Providence. That was the part, function, office, and duty in that commonwealth God took upon himself, first to foresee both his and man's joint and common good, then by his policy and legislation to bring it to pass; to make the laws, allot the posts and duties, find ways and means, lend sanction and authority. And man's duty was to obey the laws. . . .

Next *what were the laws of this kingdom?* – Some laws, you know, command and tell the subject what to do: such were those two . . . of keeping Paradise and of subduing the earth; and others forbid and tell the subject what not to do: there was in God's first kingdom one such law, the famous prohibition to eat of the Tree of Knowledge. Were there, you will ask, no other laws forbidding: none forbidding murder, theft, adultery? – None published in set terms, though murder, adultery, theft, lying were sinful and forbidden then as now; but there it lies, the bliss of that Paradise, the native virtue of that green garden, the easy constitution of that first commonwealth of God, just there it lies that no frown of God's, no stern and threatening law was needed then; for the still and private voice of conscience, reason sovereign within the heart, spoke at the right time the Yes or No and applied God's few laws to the multitude of circumstances, forbidding murder because how could man multiply if one killed another? Forbidding adultery because it was against God's institution of marriage, forbidding theft because it was against property (if in that Paradise all things were not to be common, as perhaps they were to be) and so of the rest: they were against reason, against the good of the commonwealth; that was enough, they were forbidden, they must not be. *Afterwards* the same laws were published in thunder from Mount Sinai. There were then, so far as we know, in that commonwealth but three set and spoken laws, two commanding and one forbidding, and the two first were so much in man's own nature that we might almost say there was but one, the law of the Forbidden Tree. And this law only we need consider.

What was *the forfeit for the breach of it? – Death.* . . .

For Sunday, April 25, the 4th after Easter, at St. Francis Xavier's, Liverpool

On the Gospel John 16:5–14 and in particular 8–11 (*arguet mundus de peccato et de justitia et de judicio,* etc).

. . . And when he, that is the Holy Ghost, whom our Lord in this place calls the Paraclete, *has come he will convince the world of sin and of justice and of judgment.* . . .

The first is to say what a Paraclete means. As when the Holy Ghost came on Whitsunday upon the Apostles there was heard a rush of air before the tongues of fire were seen / so when we hear this name of Paraclete our ears and minds are filled with a confused murmuring of some mystery which we know to have to do with the Holy Ghost. For God the Holy Ghost is the Paraclete, but what is a Paraclete? Often it is translated Comforter, but Paraclete does more than comfort. The word is Greek; there is no one English word for it and no one Latin word, *Comforter* is not enough. A Paraclete is one who comforts, who cheers, who encourages, who persuades, who exhorts, who stirs up, who urges forward, who calls on; what the spur and word of command is to a horse, what clapping of hands is to a speaker, what a trumpet is to the soldier, that a Paraclete is to the soul: *one who calls us on,* that is what it means, a Paraclete is one who calls us on to good. One sight is before my mind, it is homely but it comes home: you have seen at cricket how when one of the batsmen at the wicket has made a hit and wants to score a run, the other doubts, hangs back, or is ready to run in again, how eagerly the first will cry / Come on, come on! – a Paraclete is just that, something that cheers the spirit of man, with signals and with cries, all zealous that he should do something and full of assurance that if he will he can, calling him on, springing to meet him half way, crying to his ears or to his heart: This way to do God's will, this way to save your soul, come on, come on!

If this is to be a Paraclete, one who cries to the heart / Come on, no wonder Christ is a Paraclete. For he was one, he said so himself; though the Holy Ghost bears the name, yet Christ is a Paraclete too: *I will send you*, he says, *another Paraclete*, meaning that he himself was a Paraclete, the first Paraclete, the Holy Ghost the second. And did not he cry men on? Not only by words, as by his marvelous teaching and preaching; not only by standards and signals, as by his splendid miracles; but best of all by deeds, by his own example: he led the way, went before his troops, was himself the vanguard, was the forlorn hope, bore the brunt of battle alone, died upon the field, on Calvary hill and bought the victory by his blood. He cried men on; he said to his disciples, Peter and Andrew, James and John, Matthew at the custom-house, and the rest: Follow me; they did so; he warned all: He that would come after me let him deny himself and take up his cross and follow me; but when they would not follow he let them go and took all the war upon himself. *I have told you*, he said to those who came to arrest him, *that I am Jesus of Nazareth: if therefore you seek me let these go their way.*

For though Christ cheered them on they feared to follow, though the Captain led the way the soldiers fell back; he was not for that time a successful Paraclete: *all*, it says, *they all forsook him and fled.* Not that they wanted will; *the spirit was willing: Let us go too,* said Thomas, *that we may die with him;* Peter was ready to follow him to prison and to death; *but the flesh was weak:* Peter denied him in his Passion, Thomas in his resurrection, and all of them, *all forsook him and fled.* I say these things, brethren to show you that God himself may be the Paraclete, God himself may cheer men on and they too be willing to follow and yet *not* follow, not come on; something may still be wanting; and therefore Christ said: *It is for your own good that I should go; for if I do not go away the Paraclete will not come to you, whereas if I go I shall send him to you.* The second Paraclete was to do what the first did not, he was to cheer men on *and they to follow;* therefore he is called and Christ is not called *the* Paraclete.

For the feast of St. Peter and St. Paul, June 29, 1880 St. Francis Xavier's, Liverpool

A.M.D.G.

On this day, my brethren, is kept the feast of the two great Apostles Peter and Paul, in dignity the greatest of the Apostles; the one of them the rock on which the Church is built, the door-keeper to whom are given the keys of the kingdom, the Prince of the Apostles, Christ's first viceroy, the Church's first head, after Christ ascended, upon earth; the other the Apostle of the Gentiles, the great vessel of election, the twice-sevenfold mouthpiece of the Holy Ghost. They died on one day, today, by the cross and by the sword; they sealed the Gospel they preached by their blood; lovely and loveable in their lives, in death they were not divided; their sacred bodies make holy the city of Rome. Out of their lives and deaths this is the thought that tonight I shall gather: God's strength is made perfect in weakness, God that did such great things for these his two Apostles can do great things for the weakest and the worst of us here.

St. Peter was a fisherman, a poor man, a man of low degree. He could have had but little schooling even in the Law and the learning of the Jews and none at all in that of the Gentiles. He was therefore very unfit to have to dispute, as he afterwards had, out of the Law and the Prophets with men who were deeply read in them and still more was he unfit to reason with the philosophers of the Greeks, with whose philosophy and manner of reasoning he could have no acquaintance whatever. But you will say that he had at least zeal and energy, which might go far to make up for the want of learning, and that he had the priceless blessing of more than three years' constant training by Christ himself. He had, but he could not be depended on; he trusted in all this himself and fell; in the moment of trial he was found wanting, he denied his master; he said that he would die for him, but at a word from a woman he denied him and fell. His master had called him by a name that meant Rock, yet when something was to be built upon his firmness, lo, he turned to sand, the building fell and to this day, so to speak, we hear ringing the crash of it: *I tell you, I do not know the man.*

(This sermon is not to be preached either)

For Friday Evening, July 23, 1880 at St. Francis Xavier's, Liverpool

On St. Mary Magdalen, whose feast is July 22, and the love of the Sacred Heart shewn towards her (these Friday evening sermons are supposed to have to do with the Sacred Heart) as gathered chiefly from the Gospel for the feast (Luke 7:36–50).

(I preached also the Friday before, but at half an hour's notice and have no notes. The sermon was made out of an old one in this book and was on our Lord's fondness for praising and rewarding people. I thought people must be quite touched by this consideration and that I even saw some wiping their tears, but when the same thing happened next week I perceived that it was hot and that it was sweat they were wiping away.)

[Mary Magdalen] had heard of Christ, knew he was a prophet, a man come from God, a lover of men, bringing a message of forgiveness for sinners; now *she hears he is in the very town,* a chance has offered itself, mercy is at her doors, she will not let the good day, the golden opportunity slip. Christ was her good and she would make her way to it. He was dining at a Pharisee's, to that house she went.

Here see *her faith* – she knows where God is. Bad as she was she would not be blinded. She did not love darkness rather than light though her works were evil; rather she came to the light though she was to be made manifest, to be shewn a sinner, by it. But how many a heretic loves his heresy, how many a bad Catholic loves his impurity or his fraud better than the light of truth and virtue! Keeps from the church, the mass, the priest, wants to live in peace, that is in sin, even sometimes to die in peace, that is in calm despair and damnation.

Her humility: she exposes herself to the contempt of the company, to the severe judgment of Christ, to rebuff and refusal –

Her boldness: Unasked she thrusts in and while she humbles herself at Christ's feet faces the scene and the company. This humility mixed with courage or itself courage. She did what others would not have stooped to, would not have dared –

Her generosity: the rich ointment, the vessel of costly and translucent alabaster –

Her devotion, the dedication of herself to her work: her wealth first, then the hair of her own head and the kisses of her endearments of a person the beauty of which had hitherto been given over to self and to sin and to Satan.

The scene: imagine the silence, the conversation dropping off, all eyes gradually drawn to the strange spectacle, all waiting what is to follow. How will he take it? The thoughts of one we know, the host: Simon was saying to himself, 'If this man were a prophet,' etc.: he thinks Christ is detected.

At last Christ speaks: the Creditor with the Two Debtors, Simon's answer, Christ's application.

Wisdom of this answer: There is no wisdom, there is no prudence, there is no counsel against the Lord (Prov. 21:30); Simon had dug a pit and fell himself into it; the wise man was caught in his own shrewdness (1 Cor. 3:19, Job 5:13). He had thought to detect Christ and prove him no prophet, but Christ detected *him* and proved himself a prophet and more than a prophet. For he not only knew the woman was a sinner but he read Simon's secret thoughts. Though indeed his attempt to catch Christ was not a wise one, it was a piece of folly and not of wisdom; for a man may be a true prophet and yet not know everything: Balaam the prophet was a bad man and would gladly have had king Balac's gold, but he acknowledged he would say nothing but what God told him, and know nothing but what God shewed him. If then Christ had been a prophet and no more than a prophet, why was God bound to shew him whether each man and woman was just or a sinner? But Christ's answer did shew that he was a prophet and more than a prophet, a searcher of hearts.

Kindness of the answer all round: he defends Magdalen, he does not reproach Simon his host. Her he acknowledges to have been a sinner, but he makes her just; and Simon he supposes to have little sin to answer for. He does not undervalue Simon's service, for the things Simon had not done he was not expected to do; only he fully values Magdalen's and seems to say / After all you did not go so far as this.

Her reward: the forgiveness of her sins. *Remittuntur ei, etc.* Here a difficulty. Was she forgiven because she loved or did she love because she was forgiven? The words are that she was forgiven because she loved, but surely it should be the other way; for the two debtors first were forgiven and then loved. But the meaning is / Where you see in a sinner much love, as you see it in this woman, you may suppose there has been much sin, again where you know there has been much sin, as there has been in this woman, there you may expect to find much love, as here you find it; and on the other hand where there is little love shewn, as you have shown little compared with hers, there we may hope there has been little sin to forgive, and where we suppose there has been little sin, as we suppose of you, there we must not be surprised to find little love. It is then a kind of compliment to both and a warning to both; a compliment to her for her generosity, to him for his good life; a warning to her to do penance, to him to have more charity.

(And a little more. After this sermon one of my penitents told me, with great simplicity, that I was not to be named in the same week with Fr. Clare. 'Well' I said 'and I will not be named in the same week. But did you hear it all?' he said he did, only that he was sleeping for parts of it.)

For Sunday, September 12, 1880, 17th after Pentecost at St. Francis Xavier's, Liverpool

On the Gospel Matt. 22:35–46, the Answer to the Pharisees about *the Great Commandment* and the Qn. to them about *Christ the Son of David*.

When Christ our Lord, brethren, near his life's end was at the height of his renown as a prophet at Jerusalem and taught in public in the Temple / his jealous enemies, who were in the end to kill him, tried by fairer means first to put him down and overthrow his reputation. They put to him questions in public which if he did not satisfactorily answer he would be publicly discredited. And first, we read, the Pharisees sent to him their disciples with the Herodians. They did not go, the leading men among them, themselves, they would manage things if they could by a catspaw; so they send their *disciples,* as if in dispute with the Herodians, worldly men Herod's partisans; the Pharisees' disciples holding in that dispute that it was not lawful to give tribute to Caesar the Roman emperor and the others, supporters of Herod the king, who was himself supported by the favour of the emperor, maintaining that it was. To Christ they referred the question, meaning if he decided against Caesar to get him into trouble with the Roman governor and if in Caesar's favour to make him unpopular with the people. But he made such an answer as was bound to satisfy all except those whose bad purposes were baffled by it. After this came, openly and in their own persons, the Sadducees, that sect that denied the Resurrection; *they* had a question to catch Christ by, the question about the woman with the seven husbands, but by the answer he made they were themselves caught and put to silence. And the Pharisees, for they were the other great sect among the Jews, more right-thinking than the Sadducees but fuller of spiritual pride, they, you may be sure, were very glad that their rivals should have had this public encounter with Christ before themselves; for whichever way it turned out, they had said to themselves, it would be to their advantage. *They* were friends neither to the Sadducees nor to Christ: if Christ could not answer the Sadducees, there was an end of Jesus the prophet, false-prophet they called him, of Nazareth; or if Christ got the better of it, there was a blow at the Sadducees. Either way they would be the gainers. Therefore when Christ put the Sadducees to silence they were not sorry: now, they thought to themselves, he has put them down; we will put him down, and we shall have all the glory, we shall be left masters of the field.

Therefore they skillfully chose a question to put and they skillfully chose the person to put it. This was a man learned in the Law, one of themselves indeed, a Pharisee, but well inclined towards Christ and, what was much to their purpose, who could ask a question of him not captiously as if to entangle him but with a friendly and respectful manner and indeed with the sincere wish to hear Christ's judgment; for Christ, we read in St. Mark, told him that he was not far from the kingdom of God. The question therefore which he put may have been of his choosing; the Pharisees his friends may have heard it first, approved of it, and as good as said to him: Hear what the man you admire makes of this and judge him accordingly. For they thought it was one that Christ would not find easy to answer.

The question then was, as read in today's Gospel, what was the great commandment in the Law. . . .

Let us hear then Christ's answer. And fully to understand this and the scene that was taking place we must look not only at the account St. Matthew gives in today's Gospel nor at St. Mark's either but also at what St. Luke has in quite another place, where however I cannot doubt he is writing about the same event, though it suits him to change its order. Christ had to say what was the great commandment of the Law, not what *he* thought was such but to shew what it was the Law itself put forward as its great commandment. He did so: he answered the question about the Law from the Law, in the words of the Law, nay he was wiser, he went further, he got it read out from the roll of the Law by the very man that had put the question. For it would seem from St. Luke that Christ called for one of the volumes or rolls of the Law, which the Jews kept in Temple and synagogue as we keep missals in churches, unrolled it, found the place he wanted – it was the sixth chapter of the Book of Deuteronomy, the fourth and fifth verses – handed it to his questioner, and bid him read, *What is written in the Law?* He asks; *how readest thou?* that is to say / Thou shalt have the very words of the Law, here they are, read them out thyself. And here St. Mark's Gospel gives us not the sense of the passage but the very words then read: *Hear, O Israel, the Lord thy God is one God, and thou shalt love the Lord thy God with thy whole heart and with thy whole soul and with thy whole mind and with thy whole strength.* These words the lawyer read; then said Christ: *Thou hast answered rightly,* that is to say / That is the right answer and that is the first and great commandment; for the answer, you understand, was Christ's answer, *he* had found the passage, but he had made it in the Law's words and from the lawyer's lips; therefore he says, in St. Luke's account, 'Thou hast answered rightly.'

And here, brethren, you can fancy the feeling of the assembly and how at this all the hearers drew breath. There, they said to themselves, at least is an answer. And the plot, as we say, thickened, the interest and excitement heightened; for, thought they, as far as words go, as far as question and answer go, our question is answered and very clever and adroit it was of the Galilean too in the manner of its making. Only now comes the pinch, now his foot is in the trap and his own wisdom has betrayed him; *now* he has got to tell us, if this is the one great commandment, what more it is he has come to teach Israel than Israel has in the Law already. If this is the way to the Kingdom of Heaven what need have we of him to shew us the way and what right has he to tell us, as he does, that we are not already in it? What breath is there, besides, of his being the Messias in words like these? Let him leave us our great commandment and we can do without both John the Baptist and Jesus of Nazareth.

And perhaps they were coming forward again, but Christ did not allow it. He was master of the situation now. They had expected that he would add something to the great commandment, something on his own behalf: he did add something, but not what should give them fresh handles on him but what should silence them the more entirely. He had told them the first commandment, he now spoke of a second. *This,* he said, *is the first and great commandment, and the second is like it,* that is / is in keeping with it, is what you would expect from it, and follows from it. And here we may suppose he found the other place – it was from the Book of Leviticus, the nineteenth chapter and the eighteenth verse – and made the lawyer read that too: it is *Thou shalt love thy neighbor as thyself.* There was, he said, no other commandment to be compared with these two: the one was the first, the other the last, they took all duty in and on them hung all that was written in Law and Prophets.

Now the wisdom of this answer all present felt, but it acted on them in opposite ways. For as the sun, we know, melts wax and bakes clay and as one man's meat is another's poison, so Christ's answer both angered and silenced his enemies and they dared ask no more, but the lawyer whom they had put forward to question Christ and who, as I have said, was not his enemy but well disposed, he was pleased and his tongue loosened and he did ask another question even. Struck with admiration, he said that surely what Christ had taught was true and that so to love God and so to love one's neighbour was more than all holocausts and sacrifices. For, at that moment, he had an insight of the truth which when he had read the Law among his Pharisee instructors perhaps he had never seen, namely that all we do is nothing and cannot help us unless we do it for God's sake and that religion outwardly is barren unless there is charity within. And because of his wise insight Christ told him that he was not far from the Kingdom of God, giving him and all present to understand that they *did* stand in need of Christ, that they *had* something new to learn of him, nothing indeed that was not included in those two commandments, for so Christ himself allowed – *Keep these,* he said, *and live* – but nevertheless something they did not truly know, *how* to keep them. The lawyer therefore spoke again, wishing, we are told, to justify himself, that is / to become just before God and save his soul: *And who,* he asked, *is my neigh-bour?* Christ in answer told the story of the Good Samaritan, which however is not read in the Gospel of today.

So much for the best among the Pharisees, the wellmeaning one, but now for the others, for Christ's enemies. They were silenced, they were beaten, for they felt that Christ had put himself in the right and them in the wrong; he had made it appear that he kept the great commandments and they did not. For it was known, they could not deny, that he went about, seemingly at least, doing good to all men, comforting the afflicted, forgiving sinners, healing the sick, raising the dead, in all things loving his neighbour and willing to help him, including themselves the Pharisees, though himself a stranger, a Galilean, something like a Samaritan; and all this under the shew, they could not deny that it was the shew, of love and zeal for God. Whereas they, that also professed a zeal for God, they, priests and levites, were not famous for their charity to men and towards Christ in par-ticular their enmity no longer was disguised. So that he might after all be the Messias sent by God and they to blame for not receiving him. And while they stood thus sullen in their confu-sion, Christ, not to insult or triumph over them, but that being defeated they might never rally, to make his victory secure, and fasten the minds of his hearers weak in their faith and doubting, asked *them* a question in his turn, a question about the Messias. This question we will not now discuss, time does not allow, but the force of asking it was this: the Pharisees would not hear of Christ's being the promised Messias; did they then know who the Messias was to be, what he would be like, what were the marks to know him by when he should come? did they, students of the Law and the Prophets, know what the Law and the Prophets said of him and could they explain it? Christ tried them with a passage and they could not. And all who witnessed understood that there was about Messias some great mystery and that Christ who asked this question knew the secret of it, but that that was hidden from the Pharisees, according to that saying attributed to Christ: *My mystery is for me and for the children of my house.*

[In preaching I then added] You see, brethren, I have said nothing by way of exhortation to you to keep those two great commandments of the love of God and the love of your neighbour; I could not both do that and explain the Gospel, and I wanted to explain the Gospel. After all every sermon we hear, every pious book we read, everything in religion is always bidding us to keep these two commandments, on which hang the Law and the Prophets, the Old Testament and the New. My endeavour was to put before you another sample of Christ our Lord's wisdom, of the divine wisdom which dwelt in him, of the human wisdom and genius which were his as man; which think of them and study as we may we shall never reach to the bottom of, but yet by thinking of often we may come to make more of and love more every day; a blessing, etc.

Spiritual Writings

The most creative of Hopkins's spiritual writing was done during 1881–82. This was his year of tertianship. As he meditated on The Spiritual Exercises, he wrote in his journal, perhaps thinking that someday he would write a commentary on them, but this never came to fruition. He revisited his great theme, "Man was created to praise," again and again. Devlin observes Hopkins's thoughts turning from natural phenomena to a more priestly pre-occupation: "He saw creation as dependent upon the decree of the incarnation, and not the other way round. The worlds of angels and of men were created as fields for Christ in which to exercise his adoration of the Father, fields for him to sow and work and harvest. Hence, perhaps the imagery of grain and barn that ran through Hopkins's poetry, 1876–78, from 'The Wreck of the Deutschland' (stanza 31) to Poems 32 ['The Starlight Night'] and 38 ['Hurrahing in Harvest']. But after his ordination to the priesthood his interest shifted increasingly from the presence of God's design or inscape (that is, Christ) in nature to the working-out of that design – by stress and instress – in the minds and wills of men." [35]

RETREAT NOTES

The First Principle and Foundation

> Man was created to praise, reverence, and serve God Our Lord, and by so doing to save his soul. And the other things on the face of the earth were created for man's sake and to help him in the carrying out of the end for which he was created. Hence it follows that man should make use of creatures so far as they help him to attain his end and withdraw from them so far as they hinder him from so doing. For that, it is necessary to make ourselves indifferent in regard to all created things in so far as it is left to the choice of our free will and there is no prohibition; in such sort that we do not on our part seek for health rather than sickness, for riches rather than poverty, for honour rather than dishonour, for a long life rather than a short one; and so in all other things, desiring and choosing only those which may better lead us to the end for which we were created.
>
> *The Spiritual Exercises of St. Ignatius Loyola*

On "The First Principle and Foundation"

Homo Creatus Est – August 20, 1880: during this retreat, which I am making at Liverpool, I have been thinking about creation and this thought has led the way naturally through the exercises hitherto. I put down some thoughts. – We may learn that all things are created by consideration of the world without or of ourselves the world within. The former is the consideration commonly dwelt on, but the latter takes on the mind more hold. I find myself both as man and as myself something most determined and distinctive, at pitch, more distinctive and higher pitched than anything else I see; I find myself with my pleasures and pains, my powers and my experiences, my deserts and guilt, my shame and sense of beauty, my dangers, hopes, fears, and all my fate, more important to myself than anything I see. And when I ask where does all this throng and stack of being, so rich, so distinctive, so important, come from / nothing I see can answer me. And this whether I speak of human nature or of my individuality, my selfbeing. For human nature, being the more highly pitched, selved, and distinctive than anything in the world, can have been developed, evolved, condensed, from the vastness of the world not anyhow or by the working of common powers but only by one of finer or higher pitch and determination than itself and certainly than any that elsewhere we see, for this power had to force forward the starting or stubborn elements to the one pitch required. And this is much more true when we consider the mind; when I consider my selfbeing, my consciousness and feeling of myself, that taste of myself, of *I* and *me* above and in all things, which is more distinctive than the taste of ale or alum, more distinctive than the smell of walnutleaf or camphor, and is incommunicable by any means to another man. . . .

One may dwell on this further. We say that any two things however unlike are in something like. This is the one exception: when I compare my self, my being-myself, with anything else whatever, all things alike, all in the same degree, rebuff me with blank unlikeness; so that my knowledge of it, which is so intense, is from itself alone, they in no way help me to understand it. And even those things with which I in some sort identify myself, as my country or family, and those things which I own and call mine, as my clothes and so on, all presuppose the stricter sense of *self* and *me* and *mine* and are from that derivative. . . .

Notes from a Long Retreat

November–December 1881. For being required to adore God and enter into a covenant of justice with him [Lucifer] did so indeed, but, as a chorister who learns by use in the church itself the strength and beauty of his voice, he became aware in his very note of adoration of the riches of his nature; then when from that first note he should have gone on with the sacrificial service, prolonging the first note instead and ravished by his own sweetness and dazzled, the prophet says, by his beauty, he was involved in spiritual sloth . . . and spiritual luxury and vainglory; to heighten this, he summoned a train of spirits to be his choir and, contemptuously breaking with the service of the Eucharistic sacrifice, which was to have a victim of earthly nature and of flesh, raise a hymn in honour of their own nature, spiritual purely and ascending, he must have persuaded them, to the divine; and with this sin of pride aspiring to godhead their crime was consummated. . . .

This song of Lucifer's was a dwelling on his own beauty, an instressing of his own inscape, and like a performance on the organ and instrument of his own being; it was sounding, as they say, of his own trumpet and a hymn in his own praise. . . .

Clearly, Hopkins recognized that he faced the same danger. How could a poet avoid self-consciousness in praising God? American poet Paul Mariani writes: "Part of the answer is offered in Hopkins's sonnet on Henry Purcell: the singer must keep his attention riveted on the realization of the object. If he does this and does it well, something of his own distinctive individuality will flash or ripple off the song in the act of its being sung. If the singer begins to dwell on his own singing, however, his song falters, becomes cacophonous, fails. Then it is one's "sweating self" and not the other *that occupies the central space of the poem/song, and both singer and song fall.*"[36]

Further Notes on the Foundation

August 7 1882. God's utterance of himself in himself is God the Word, outside himself is this world. This world then is word, expression, news of God. Therefore its end, its purpose, its purport, its meaning, is God and its life or work to name and praise him. Therefore praise put before reverence and service. . . .

On Personality, Grace, and Free Will

Besides the above stated distinction of freedom of pitch and freedom of play there is a third kind of freedom still to be considered, *freedom of field.* (This is the natural order of the three: freedom of pitch that is / self-determination, is in the chooser himself and his choosing faculty; freedom of play is in the execution; freedom of field is in the object, the field of choice.) Thus it is freedom of play to be free of some benevolent man's purse, to have access to it at your will; it is freedom of pitch to be allowed to take from it what you want, not to be limited by conditions of his imposing; it is freedom of field to find there *more than one coin to choose from.* Or it is freedom of pitch to be able to choose for yourself which of several doors you will go in by; it is freedom of play to go unhindered to it and through the one you choose; but suppose all were false doors or locked but the very one you happened to choose and you do not know it, there is here wanting freedom of field. . . .

God can always command if he choose the free consent of the elective will, at least, if by no other way, by shutting out all freedom of field (which no doubt does sometimes take place, as in disposing the hearts of princes; but whether in matters concerning the subject's own salvation we do not know: very possibly it does in answer to the subject's own or some other's prayer in his behalf). Therefore in that 'cleave' of being which each of his creatures shows to God's eyes alone (or in its 'burl' of being / uncloven) God can choose countless points in the strain (or countless cleaves of the 'burl') where the creature has consented, does consent, to God's will in the way above shewn. But these may be away, may be very far away, from the actual pitch at any given moment existing. It is into that possible world that God for the moment moves his creature out of this one or it is from that possible world that he brings his creature into this, shewing it to itself gracious and consenting; nay more, clothing its old self for the moment with a gracious and consenting self. This shift is grace. For grace is any action, activity, on God's part by which, in creating or after creating, he carries the creature to or towards the end of its being, which is its selfsacrifice to God and its salvation. . . .

Prayer is the expression of a wish to God and, since God searches the heart, the conceiving even of the wish is prayer in God's eyes (see Rom. 8:26, 27). For there must be something which shall be truly the creature's in the work of corresponding with grace: this is the *arbitrium,* the verdict on God's side, the saying Yes, the 'doing-agree' (so to speak barbarously), and looked at in itself, such a nothing is the creature before its creator, it is found to be no more than the mere wish, discernible by God's eyes, that it might do as he wishes, might correspond, might say Yes to him; correspondence itself is on man's side not so much corresponding as the wish to correspond, and this least sigh of desire, this one aspiration, is the life and spirit of man. . . .

Creation and Redemption the Great Sacrifice

The first intention then of God outside himself or, as they say, *ad extra,* outwards, the first outstress of God's power, was Christ; and we must believe that the next was the Blessed Virgin. Why did the Son of God go thus forth from the Father not only in the external and intrinsic procession of the Trinity but also by an extrinsic and less than eternal, let us say aeonian one? – To give God glory and that by sacrifice, sacrifice offered in the barren wilderness outside of God, as the children of Israel were led into the wilderness to offer sacrifice. This sacrifice and this outward procession is a consequence and shadow of the procession of the Trinity, from which mystery sacrifice takes its rise; but of this I do not mean to write here. It is as if the blissful agony or stress of selving in God had forced out drops of sweat or blood, which drops were the world. . . .

In going forth to do sacrifice Christ went not alone but created angels to be his company, lambs to follow him the Lamb, the flower of the flock, 'whithersoever he went', that is to say, first to the hill of sacrifice, then after that back to God, to beatitude. They were to take part in the sacrifice and he was to redeem them all, that is to say / for the sake of the Lamb of God who was God himself God would accept the whole flock and for the sake of one ear or grape the whole sheaf or cluster; for redeem may be said not only of the recovering from sin to grace or perdition to salvation but also of the raising from worthlessness before God (and all creation is unworthy of God) to worthiness of him, the meriting of God himself, or, so to say, godworthiness. . . .

Retreat at Beaumont, September 8, 1883

During this retreat I have much and earnestly prayed that God will lift me above myself to a higher state of grace, in which I may have more union with him, be more zealous to do his will, and freer from sin. Yesterday night it was 15 years exactly since I came to the Society. . . .

Also in some meditation today I earnestly asked our Lord to watch over my compositions, not to preserve them from being lost or coming to nothing, for that I am very willing they should be, but that they might not do me harm through the enmity or imprudence of any man or my own; that he should have them as his own and employ or not employ them as he would see fit. And this I believe is heard.

PART V

Wrestling with God

HOPKINS RELUCTANTLY MOVED to Dublin on February 18, 1884, into two yoked houses that had fallen from neoclassic Georgian splendor, from ornamental pastel plaster and stucco work, to crudely divided rooms painted chocolate brown. Hopkins came to teach Greek and Latin at University College, in a town whose two main industries were Guinness beer and whiskey. Upon his arrival, he sent birthday wishes to John Henry Newman, "from where I never thought to be, in a University for Catholic Ireland begun under your leadership, which has since those days indeed long and unhappily languished. . . . In the events which have brought me here I recognise the hand of providence, but nevertheless have felt and feel an unfitness which led me at first to try to decline the offer made me and now does not yet allow my spirits to rise to the level of the position and its duties. . . ." The Jesuit residence to which Hopkins, six months before his fortieth birthday, was posted at 85–86 St. Stephen's Green was in disrepair; the leaky plumbing and polluted drains would cause his death five years later from typhoid. Catherine Phillips writes:

> The college had been expanded from a small "cramming" institution and moved in November 1883 into the crumbling buildings of the Catholic University founded by Newman in the 1850s. . . .

Father Delaney, the moving power behind the formation of the new college, wanted to establish a Catholic rival to the Protestant Trinity College. . . . Despite vehement opposition Delaney managed to secure university funds for posts in classics and mathematics. . . . For the classicist Delaney decided that there were no Irish scholars appropriate and sought an English Jesuit. The post was offered to Hopkins. Letters exchanged by Father Delaney and Father Purbrick, the Provincial of the English province, show confidence in Hopkins's classical knowledge but . . . acknowledged difficulty in finding appropriate employment for him.[37]

Norman White says, in his meticulous study, *Hopkins in Ireland*:

Most of the college's activities took place in 86, a square block of a Georgian mansion, called by Delany a "neglected old barracks" (Newman was probably the first to describe it as a "barracks," and the description stuck). It was full of dry rot, and sanitary arrangements were outdated and unhygienic; despite frequent requests the bishops would not allocate funds for repairs which the Jesuits could not afford . . . there were few books, professors having to buy whatever was offered in the bookshops on the Liffey quays. As there was nowhere to house the books, they were arranged on various staircase-landings.[38]

White characterizes Dublin after 1884 as

a deposed capital in economic decline. . . . Impoverished, unhealthy, and gloomy. . . . Idle servants and other dependents of the departed civilisation joined the increasing numbers of peasants coming in from the country, to create large-scale unemployment, poverty, and misery. . . . The major social problems included drunkenness and ill-health. Country people were afraid to visit the city because of the high mortality rate from infectious diseases. . . . The river Liffey was the city's major sewer, and house drains were in an appalling state, particularly those of properties on low-lying soil.

St. Stephen's Green was low-lying and the drains of No. 86 were infested with rats. "The house we are in, the College," wrote Hopkins, "is a sort of ruin."[39]

Hopkins was miserable. He wrote to his mother, "It is impossible to say what a mess Ireland is and how everything enters into that mess. The college is . . . rather a failure than a success, and there is less prospect of success now than before. . . . Here too, unless things are to change, I labour for what is worth little. And in doing this most fruitless work I use up all opportunity of doing any other." He also wrote to Bridges of his new teaching position: "It is an honour and an opening and has many bright sides, but at present it has also some dark ones and this in particular that I am not at all strong, not strong enough for the requirements. . . ."

Hopkins kept "The Dublin Notebook," which Norman White describes as "a battered red exercise book which also gives evidence in a most raw and direct way of his disturbed consciousness in 1884."[40] In this notebook, Hopkins recorded the bad translations his students produced. "Hopkins was shocked by the poor standard of examination answers – most would appear to him to be of elementary-school rather than university quality – and the general standard of written literacy, particularly grammar and spelling, would have been inferior to that in England."[41] White quotes some amusing examples of Hopkins's students' translations of a Latin phrase:

> So good a gladiator though certainly rude
> Was so good a gladiator so vulgar with his food?
> So good a gladiator get red suddenly!
> A good rough gladiator though hasty.[42]

In March, Hopkins's new pen pal, Coventry Patmore, finally, after nearly a month, responded to Hopkins's poems. His reaction echoed everyone else's – Patmore wrote that the poems "appeal only to the few," and that he "could never become sufficiently accustomed to your favorite poem, 'The Wreck of the Deutschland,' to reconcile me to its strangenesses." Patmore then told Robert Bridges that he found Hopkins extremely appealing both as a man and as a genius, but that he found his poetry alien. To compound the disappointment that his friend's reactions must have caused him, life in Dublin was "at an ebb," Hopkins wrote to Bridges, and the weather worse than anything he ever experienced in England. He added later that he was "recovering from a deep fit of nervous prostration. . . . I did not know but I was dying."

In late summer, after a "circular ticket" allowed him to tour most of Ireland, Hopkins began his extraordinary sonnet "Spelt from Sybil's Leaves," a semi-apocalyptic *Dies Irae*[43] that would require two more years to finish. He looked up at the darkening sky: "Evening strains to be time's vast, womb-of-all, home-of-all, hearse-of-all night." Next he wrote a relatively plain-style sonnet which begins "To seem the stranger lies my lot, my life / Among strangers" and ends "I am in Ireland now; now I am at a third / Remove. . . . / This to hoard unheard, / Heard unheeded, leaves me a lonely began." He was unpopular and unpragmatic as a teacher, whose students rarely attended his classes, except occasionally to learn what would not appear on the examinations. He described himself as "drowning" in the grading of hundreds and hundreds of exams. "I wake and feel the fell of dark, not day," he opened one sonnet; "I am gall, I am heartburn," he continued. He wrote a letter about his friend Geldart's suicide. Within two years of this, his final professional assignment, he composed more "terrible sonnets": "Not, I'll not carrion comfort, Despair, not feast on thee. . . ." And so, in Dublin, Hopkins came to exemplify a concentrated version of himself: asceticism embraced by a wildly original nature; self-invented avoidance of poetry; the poet who destroyed his writings when he joined the Jesuits; the depressed priest who renounced his own genius to serve an unsuitable vocation: all of these images form the now-familiar tale of Gerard Manley Hopkins's conflicted, hidden life.

And yet, in Ireland, he did resort to poetry to do that which he could do in no other way – he called it "fetching out" God, greeting him "the days I meet him," grabbing and then releasing highly inventive meetings with God in the strangest places – not just in birds and stars and clouds, but in a shipwreck, a trout covered with moles, a dead farrier, an emotional breakdown. By the final years of his short life, Hopkins seems to have understood that he had an obligation, a responsibility, to spell God out. The much-discussed conflict between Hopkins's natural character as a connoisseur of beauty and his career as a slum-dwelling, scrupulously obedient servant of his insensitive superiors came home to roost in his last five years in Dublin. He was often and then fatally sick, responding to God not in nature, but in his own personal desolation. The sonnets of these Dublin years provide impeccably managed and edited examples of mature poetic genius.

Seamus Heaney said that Hopkins had "the horse sense of a poet hiding in the cellar of a Jesuit." He said that in everything Hopkins composed, you could "graph the intensity." One can also see that Hopkins held contending ideas about his own poetic undertakings. Norman White's position throughout his *Hopkins: A Literary Biography* suggests that Hopkins's genius suffered from his self-bridling. While describing Hopkins's poems as "some of the most remarkable works of art ever produced,"[44] White also points out that:

> Hopkins's powerful and original temperament, a strange mixture of innocence and expertise, of old prejudices and clear-sighted

observations, worked against his achieving happiness and success. It constantly expressed itself in enthusiasms and antipathies rather than calm appraisals. He adored or hated his environments; his reactions to place and to the lack of a settled home are centrally important to Hopkins and his poetry. He sometimes despaired at his apparent inability to control himself and his destiny. His solutions were typically impractical and extreme. He attempted to simplify his problems and evade his demons by complete submission to ancient comprehensive ideological systems; he became a Roman Catholic and then a Jesuit.[45]

René Gallet challenges White's statement that "there can be no doubt about the conflict between the priest and the poet,"[46] which summarizes the almost universal opinion held by Hopkins's critical readers. Gallet questions the consensus that Hopkins was simply conflicted about writing poetry. He claims:

> The thesis of the priest-poet conflict, expressed in such vivid terms, assumes a particular view of poetry. In Hopkins's case this is felt to be an irrepressible impulse ("Hopkins was a compulsive poet: even repressed by a severely ascetic moral culture, his compulsiveness created space for itself").[47] The type of inner conflict outlined here is largely the result of a simplifying, if not partly inaccurate, construction. . . . The problem as stated by Hopkins concerns not so much poetic composition as the "hopes for fame." . . . The fact that he should spontaneously include the fate of his poems in his prayers during a retreat hardly favors the theory that he felt his creation to be fundamentally at odds with his spiritual life, though the latter clearly took precedence.[48]

Although no one today would imagine describing Hopkins as a failure – he tops the lists of great poets, literary innovators, and linguistic revolutionaries, and can be regarded as a spiritual master – the man himself suffered throughout his Catholic years in a state of disappointment (that his scholarship was not encouraged by the Society of Jesus), with a sense of failure (he was unpopular as a preacher and teacher), and frustration (as a poet, he felt unproductive and unloved).

During his years as an ordained priest, and even after he wrote his first great poem as a Jesuit, Hopkins considered his religious endeavors to be of the highest order of importance. While admiring Christ for "the holding of himself back," and criticizing the Romantic poets for revealing an excess of ego, he also regretted in his letters to Bridges and Dixon that he himself seemed unable to breed a "work that wakes." Like all Jesuits, he was supposed to work at all things *Ad Majoram Dei Gloria* – for the greater glory of God. And this he did. He demonstrated that nature signified to him something like the body of God. This significance fed into every poem he wrote. His euphoria in apprehending divine presence in nature, alternating with his despondency at divine distance from his own soul, also marked his work. One could say that he had a love-hate relationship with poetry – he loved the God he could instress while watching a falcon glide, and best expressed that love in a great poem. But in his letters, at least, he redundantly wondered whether poetry could coexist with his priesthood – ministering to the predominantly poor flock, delivering unpopular sermons, and grading thousands of high school Latin exams each academic year.

On the other hand, many readers – including René Gallet, quoted above – challenge the well-worn opinion that Hopkins suffered from a constant conflict between his two vocations. Some have recognized Hopkins's achievement of consolation in the last poems of his life. In the "terrible sonnets," we certainly encounter his sadness, isolation, and stubborn inability to submit – to let go, let God: "No worst, there is none"; "Comforter, where, where is your comforting?"; "I wretch." While selving as Hopkins conceived of it – as an unselfconscious performance of divinely created individuality – was ideal, self-taste in his late sonnets becomes bitter, gall, and heartburn: "The lost are like this, and their scourge to be / As I am mine, their sweating selves; but worse."

Hopkins traveled a long and hypersensitive path of austerity and even nervous collapse before reaching what Ignatius calls, and many readers detect in Hopkins, "a state of consolation." In his review of Paul Mariani's biography of Hopkins in *The New Yorker,* Brad Leithauser says:

> We can't help but feel . . . comforted – to see a soul in extremis still creating brilliant wordplay, still working thrilling variations into the sonnet form. . . . I cannot imagine any future . . . in which readers will not find solace at the thought of the anguished man taking such scrupulous care with the formal demands of the sonnet even while extravagantly innovating with meter and diction and syntax. Those strange rhythms of Hopkins are a heartbeat that fibrillates wildly.[49]

Decades after his death, Hopkins became suddenly and then increasingly recognized for a poetic product which not only influenced countless writers who came after, but also articulated a religious vocation that served the greater glory of God through art.

It is hard to connect Hopkins's powerful writing with the image that comes down to us of him as a Jesuit – delicate, highly strung, frail. One Jesuit remembered him grading papers at three in the morning, sobbing uncontrollably with his head wrapped in wet towels. Another Jesuit, a lay brother, reported that he thought Fr. Hopkins (the Double-First, whom Benjamin Jowett called the Star of Balliol) was simple-minded. He suffered chronically from eyestrain, headaches, and anemia. He hated teaching and loathed giving sermons. He seemed to have no gift for pastoral work. But this slight, exhausted priest – who felt himself a failure – almost without wanting to, produced a most extraordinary opus.

Hopkins always possessed strongly melancholic tendencies. Norman White concurs:

> Hopkins's life . . . was an unpatterned succession of turmoils, sometimes with an apparently unsuccessful climax which did not fulfill its promise or which led to contradictory outcomes. . . . "The Wreck of the Deutschland," his first great artistic achievement, was immediately followed by its official rejection. . . . His "salad days" in Wales ended with the failure of his theology examination; the subsequent unsettled period as "Fortune's football" was at last relieved by a permanent posting, but this proved the one from which he most needed change. His time in Dublin of near madness and despair was calmed only by his death. . . . Finally in Ireland a new power and kind of originality were forced into his poetics of self-examination by diminished loyalties and many dimensions of isolation.[50]

During Hopkins's final five years in Ireland his poems, written sparsely before he died at age forty-four, seem to echo the familiar words of Psalm 130: "Out of the depths have I cried unto thee, O Lord."

Philip Endean, SJ, points out that though Hopkins may well have been personally unsuited to his religious vocation, that same vocation outfitted him with a vocabulary and a discipline that combined to create ultimate greatness. Here Fr. Endean refers to Hopkins's sonnet, written while serving as a pastor among the poor in 1880, about ministering to the dying farrier, Felix Randal:

> The nervous, bookish curate and the brawny blacksmith cannot have had much in common, and if Hopkins served Felix, it was

not through poetic talent. The poem itself is a private reflection on priestly ministry and is not itself and never could be a priestly act. . . . It is possible that Hopkins made a terrible mistake . . . and that he had no vocation for the priesthood. If this is so, it also has to be said that Ignatian spirituality enabled him to find a sacramental vision that led to great religious poetry in a way that no other religious influence in Victorian England could have done. It is possible to see [in his texts] God drawing him toward himself.[51]

As a poet and as a person, Hopkins was prone to desolation. As a Christian and as a priest, he claims repeatedly to have experienced consolation. How could he fuse these dialectical tendencies? The poems and even the prose of his final five years stand apart from his earlier work. Marked by a raw confessional quality, the poems have been called alternately the "terrible sonnets" or "the sonnets of desolation." Composed when crushing exhaustion, depression, and unwelcome pressure reached a climax, these writings also express a final breakthrough.

He had written to Robert Bridges that poetry was "unprofessional"; he had written to Canon Dixon that "my vocation puts before me a standard so high that a higher can be found nowhere else," leading Hopkins to claim that he must leave the use of his talent entirely at God's "disposal." Quite probably the religious perfection that Hopkins sought in the strictness of the Jesuit discipline and the poetic perfection he found in his own extraordinary metrical feats united in a new and sudden way in the last poems of his life. Moral power and blunt honesty added profundity to the flash and dazzle of his earlier poems. Thus did his "terrible sonnets" address the most intimate and compelling problems of his or any spiritual life.

Hopkins's last poems also reveal his loneliness, which in his case included an isolation of mind as well as a condition of solitude. He had written to Bridges, "You give me a long jobation about eccentricities. Alas, I have heard so much about and suffered so much for in fact been so completely ruined for life by my alleged singularities that they are a sore subject." True – in almost every peculiarity they have reported, Hopkins's biographers have dwelled on his willfulness and scrupulosity: how he abstained from water until he almost died when he was a schoolboy; how he insisted against ponderous objection on becoming a Roman Catholic; how he sought within the Jesuits an exactitude and rigor of observance that caused his superiors to bid him cease; how he punished his verse to make every line just so – and just so revolutionary.

In the summer of 1888, with less than a year left to live, Hopkins began an ambitious twenty-four-line "sonnet" with a complex philosophical title: "That Nature is a Heraclitean Fire and the Comfort of the Resurrection." In August he wrote to Bridges from Scotland: "I will now go to bed, the more so as I am going to preach tomorrow and put plainly to a Highland congregation of MacDonalds, Mackintoshes, Mackillops, and the rest what I am putting not at all so plainly to the rest of the world, or rather to you and Canon Dixon, in a sonnet in sprung rhythm with two codas." And in September:

> Lately I sent you a sonnet on the Heraclitean Fire, in which a great deal of early Greek philosophical thought was distilled; but the liquor of the distillation did not taste very Greek, did it? The effect of studying masterpieces is to make me admire and do otherwise. So it must be on every original artist to some degree, on me to a marked degree. Perhaps then more reading would only refine my singularity, which is not what you want.

As an undergraduate, Hopkins had studied pre-Socratic philosophy with his tutor, Benjamin Jowett. Heraclitus, sixth century BCE, argued, against the received notions of his day, for the unity of human experience, the constancy of change, and the dominance of fire above the three other natural elements. In Dublin, in his last year, pale and exhausted, visited by "fits of sadness so severe they resemble madness," Hopkins turned his attention to an obscure pre-Christian Greek philosopher to support his experience. The result was a most incredible poem. "That Nature is a Heraclitean Fire" begins with a rehearsal of images that we have seen before in Hopkins's work – cloud puffballs, throng, marches, shadowtackles, ropes, wrestles, toil, footfretted – all familiar. But line nine expresses a consensus: "million fuelèd, nature's bonfire burns on."

Ultimately, man and nature are reduced and united as "trash" and "ash." "All is in an enormous dark / Drowned" and "Manshape . . . death blots black out." Hopkinsian nature, idiosyncratically recorded, followed by man trashed, suddenly erupts with a new idea: The Resurrection. Then:

> Across my foundering deck shone
> A beacon, an eternal beam. | Flesh fade, and mortal trash
> Fall to the residuary worm; | world's wildfire, leave but ash:
>   In a flash, at a trumpet crash,
> I am all at once what Christ is, | since he was what I am, and
> This Jack, joke, poor potsherd, | patch, matchwood, immortal
>   diamond

Out of unimaginable pressure, diamond emerges. And these two words appear on Hopkins's stone in Poets' Corner, Westminster Abbey: "Immortal diamond."

Still, Hopkins's suffering did not evaporate. He would write more sonnets which were more or less "terrible." Weary to the point of illness, Hopkins in Dublin seemed able to scruple no more, and though eventually he would complain, "Sweet fire the sire of muse, my soul needs this; / I want the one rapture of an inspiration," he had in fact brought forth the amazing and terrible sonnets. In these last poems, an authentic voice echoes the voice of his letters, in spare, sere confessions. There is no elaborate indirectness of speech. They address God informally – "O thou my friend" – and cry out for comfort. For the first time in his life, Hopkins asks for mercy, and he asks it of God. In their intense relationship to God, these poems actually avoid the sin of despair.

St. Ignatius describes desolation as a predictable part of the spiritual journey, as "darkness of soul, turmoil of spirit, inclination to what is low and earthly, restlessness rising from many disturbances and temptations which lead to want of faith, want of hope, want of love." That Hopkins in his last sonnets details those "wants" reveals a new poetic persona. And so the "terrible sonnets" express not despair, and not even total desolation, but rather, self-revulsion, and desperate yearning to be heard. Significantly, Hopkins as the priest is using poetry as the medium of his most powerful prayer.

Hopkins wrote that these last sonnets came to him "unbidden and against my will." As he stopped trying to separate his ascetic morality from his poetic impulses, his writing became flooded with the moral insight that twenty years of conscientious study of *The Spiritual Exercises* had bestowed upon him. In these poems his characteristic consciousness of nature, his acute intelligence about poetry, and his theological training were joined by a new element – his personal daily relations with God, relations which were clearly not without vexation.

Critics have easily contrasted the dark tone and matter of these last sonnets with the buoyant nature poems that he wrote between "The Wreck of the Deutschland" (1875–6) and his move to Dublin in 1884. After relocating, the process by which Hopkins came to grasp the whole world – and himself within it – as a living sacrament of divine presence, forced the lashing and flaming of nature into the background and his own personality to the foreground.

Three months before he died, on June 8, 1889, Hopkins composed his sonnet "Thou art indeed just, Lord," which exemplifies more than any other single expression of his life his perception of the interdependence of his two vocations as priest and poet. The poem opens with a quotation from Jeremiah: "Thou, indeed, O Lord, art just, if I plead with thee, but yet I will speak what is just to thee: Why doth the way of the wicked prosper? Why is it well with all them that transgress and do wickedly?" (Jer. 12:1). While on a retreat the year before he wrote this sonnet, Hopkins had noted in his journal:

> I began to enter on that course of loathing and hopelessness which I have so often felt before which made me fear madness. . . . What is my wretched life? . . . I wish then for death; yet if I died now I should die imperfect, no master of myself, and this is the worst failure of all. O my God, look down on me.

Three days after writing these retreat notes he sent a letter to Bridges, "all impulse fails me: I can give myself no sufficient reason for going on. Nothing comes: I am a eunuch – but it is for the kingdom of heaven's sake." Hopkins at this point had given up the practice of meditation out of fear of madness, and now that he was required to meditate in retreat, the result of his introspection was the question, "What is my wretched life?"

In the earlier "terrible sonnets," Hopkins associates introspection with darkness, wretchedness, gall, bitterness, sourness, eating carrion. The progression of "I wretch lay wrestling with (my God!) my God" to "God's most deep decree / Bitter would have me taste: my taste was me" to "let joy size / At God knows when to God knows what" reveals an ongoing movement, the bitterness of self-determination, and the effort at detachment of will. By the time Hopkins writes "Thou art indeed just, Lord," he seems to synthesize his interactions with God with his own selving.

In a letter to Bridges dated March 20, 1889, about ten weeks before Hopkins's death, he included the sonnet "Thou art indeed just, Lord." One can imagine Bridges – established, wealthy, optimistic, leisured, attacking the sonnet for both its difficult rhetoric and distressing content, and one can equally imagine Hopkins being "rather bitter." Five weeks later, he sent "To R. B." a poem whose last lines are:

> O then if in my lagging lines you miss
> The roll, the rise, the carol, the creation,
> My winter world, that scarcely breathes that bliss
> Now yields you, with some sighs, our explanation.

This turned out to be the last poem he would write and his last correspondence with Bridges – a touching, though apparently unsuccessful, final attempt at self-explanation.

When Bridges wrote to Dixon on June 14, 1889, announcing Hopkins's death, he included a revealing postscript: "That dear Gerard was overworked, unhappy, and would never have done anything great seems to give no solace. But how much worse it would have been had his promise of performance been more splendid. He seems to have been entirely lost and destroyed, by those Jesuits." How unjust that a life so brilliant should seem "entirely lost and destroyed," not only to its bearer, but even to his best friend. Bridges's postscript seems a fit gloss to his understanding of Hopkins's "terrible sonnets." In fact, though Hopkins suffered deeply, he insisted throughout that he felt himself in consonance with God's will, and that this feeling was to him better than "violets knee-deep." Not everyone personally experiences God's will, but Hopkins did. This plaintive sonnet to Bridges provides a monument to the integration of that experience with personal suffering.

God's justice often bewilders human beings, and the rain falls on the just and the unjust alike. In "Thou are indeed just," Hopkins engages God in a colloquy, wondering why, if he as God's friend is defeated and thwarted, do sinners prosper? This is not the question of a jealous or self-righteous Pharisee, but rather of one who compares himself to the rest of the world and finds himself stagnant. Nature is productive: "banks and brakes" are "lacéd" with "fretty chervil" (cow parsley), "and fresh wind shakes them." "Birds build, but not I build. . . ." No wind of inspiration helps speed the contending speaker, who spends life, strains, and does not breed. Birds build nests, but Hopkins has no nest. "Work that wakes," which he would like to breed, means not only a work that will last, but one that arouses a life of its own separate from his weary self. Once again he refers to himself as a "eunuch." Still and dry, deprived of fluency, lubrication, and flow of water, symbolic in nature and throughout the Bible, he humbly but plainly begs, "Mine, O thou Lord of life, send my roots rain."

The tone of this request is not wretched or writhing, like the tone of the previous dark sonnets. Emphasis instead falls on the word "Mine," implying Hopkins's possessive intimacy with the "Lord of life." And since life – vitality, growth, inspiration, movement – is what he requests in "send my roots rain," and not the sleep of death, this is surely a hopeful poem. Previous intimations of hope and consolation invariably fluctuated and proved insufficient. But here, at last, at the very end of his career, his poetry marks a great talent aligning itself with a great will.

Poetry is the sacrament of word and spirit, charged upward by interpenetration with each other. When Hopkins's resistance broke, when he himself broke, his highest gift was released.

beech, godshill church wind
fr Appleducombe
July 25.

Poems

(1884–1889)

Spelt from Sibyl's Leaves

Earnest, earthless, equal, attuneable, | vaulty, voluminous, . . .
  stupendous
Evening strains to be tíme's vást, | womb-of-all, home-of-all,
  hearse-of-all night.
Her fond yellow hornlight wound to the west, | her wild hollow
  hoarlight hung to the height
Waste; her earliest stars, earl-stars, | stárs principal, overbend us,
Fíre-féaturing heaven. For earth | her being has unbound, her
  dapple is at an end, as-
tray or aswarm, all throughther, in throngs; | self ín self steepèd
  and páshed – qúite
Disremembering, dísmémbering | áll now. Heart, you round me
  right
With: Óur évening is over us; óur night | whélms, whélms, ánd
  will end us.
Only the beak-leaved boughs dragonish | damask the tool-
  smooth bleak light; black,
Ever so black on it. Óur tale, O óur oracle! | Lét life, wáned, ah lét
  life wind
Off hér once skéined stained véined varíety | upon, áll on twó
  spools; párt, pen, páck
Now her áll in twó flocks, twó folds – black, white; | right, wrong;
  reckon but, reck but, mind
But thése two; wáre of a wórld where bút these | twó tell, each off
  the óther; of a rack
Where, selfwrung, selfstrung, sheathe- and shelterless, | thóughts
  agaínst thoughts ín groans grínd.

To seem the stranger lies my lot, my life

To seem the stranger lies my lot, my life
Among strangers. Father and mother dear,
Brothers and sisters are in Christ not near
And he my peace my parting, sword and strife.
    England, whose honour O all my heart woos, wife
To my creating thought, would neither hear
Me, were I pleading, plead nor do I: I wear-
y of idle a being but by where wars are rife.

    I am in Ireland now; now I am at a third
Remove. Not but in all removes I can
Kind love both give and get. Only what word
Wisest my heart breeds dark heaven's baffling ban
Bars or hell's spell thwarts. This to hoard unheard,
Heard unheeded, leaves me a lonely began.

I wake and feel the fell of dark, not day

I wake and feel the fell of dark, not day.
What hours, O what black hoürs we have spent
This night! what sights you, heart, saw; ways you went!
And more must, in yet longer light's delay.

      With witness I speak this. But where I say
Hours I mean years, mean life. And my lament
Is cries countless, cries like dead letters sent
To dearest him that lives alas! away.

    I am gall, I am heartburn. God's most deep decree
Bitter would have me taste: my taste was me;
Bones built in me, flesh filled, blood brimmed the curse.
    Selfyeast of spirit a dull dough sours. I see
The lost are like this, and their scourge to be
As I am mine, their sweating selves; but worse.

No worst, there is none. Pitched past pitch of grief

No worst, there is none. Pitched past pitch of grief,
More pangs will, schooled at forepangs, wilder wring.
Comforter, where, where is your comforting?
Mary, mother of us, where is your relief?
My cries heave, herds-long; huddle in a main, a chief
Woe, world-sorrow; on an age-old anvil wince and sing –
Then lull, then leave off. Fury had shrieked 'No ling-
ering! Let me be fell: force I must be brief'.

O the mind, mind has mountains; cliffs of fall
Frightful, sheer, no-man-fathomed. Hold them cheap
May who ne'er hung there. Nor does long our small
Durance deal with that steep or deep. Here! creep,
Wretch, under a comfort serves in a whirlwind: all
Life death does end and each day dies with sleep.

Carrion Comfort

Not, I'll not, carrion comfort, Despair, not feast on thee;
Not untwist – slack they may be – these last strands of man
In me ór, most weary, cry *I can no more* I can;
Can something, hope, wish day come, not choose not to be.
But ah, but O thou terrible, why wouldst thou rude on me
Thy wring-world right foot rock? lay a lionlimb against me? scan
With darksome devouring eyes my bruisèd bones? and fan,
O in turns of tempest, me heaped there; me frantic to avoid thee
    and flee?

Why? That my chaff might fly; my grain lie, sheer and clear.
Nay in all that toil, that coil, since (seems) I kissed the rod,
Hand rather, my heart lo! lapped strength, stole joy, would laugh,
    chéer.
Cheer whom though? the hero whose heaven-handling flung me,
    fóot tród
Me? or me that fought him? O which one? is it each one? That
    night, that year
Of now done darkness I wretch lay wrestling with (my God!) my
    God.

Patience, hard thing! the hard thing but to pray

Patience, hard thing! the hard thing but to pray,
But bid for, Patience is! Patience who asks
Wants war, wants wounds; weary his times, his tasks;
To do without, take tosses, and obey.
　　Rare patience roots in these, and, these away,
Nowhere. Natural heart's ivy, Patience masks
Our ruins of wrecked past purpose. There she basks
Purple eyes and seas of liquid leaves all day.

　　We hear our hearts grate on themselves: it kills
To bruise them dearer. Yet the rebellious wills
Of us we do bid God bend to him even so.
　　And where is he who more and more distils
Delicious kindness? – He is patient. Patience fills
His crisp combs, and that comes those ways we know.

My own heart let me more have pity on

My own heart let me more have pity on; let
Me live to my sad self hereafter kind,
Charitable; not live this tormented mind
With this tormented mind tormenting yet.
    I cast for comfort I can no more get
By groping round my comfortless, than blind
Eyes in their dark can day or thirst can find
Thirst's all-in-all in all a world of wet.

Soul, self; come, poor Jackself, I do advise
You, jaded, let be; call off thoughts awhile
Elsewhere; leave comfort root-room; let joy size
At God knows when to God knows what; whose smile
's not wrung, see you; unforeseen times rather – as skies
Betweenpie mountains – lights a lovely mile.

Tom's Garland:
Upon the Unemployed

Tom – garlanded with squat and surly steel
Tom; then Tom's fallowbootfellow piles pick
By him and rips out rockfire homeforth – sturdy Dick;
Tom Heart-at-ease, Tom Navvy: he is all for his meal
Sure,'s bed now. Low be it: lustily he his low lot (feel
That ne'er need hunger, Tom; Tom seldom sick,
Seldomer heartsore; that treads through, prickproof, thick
Thousands of thorns, thoughts) swings though. Commonweal
Little I reck ho! lacklevel in, if all had bread:
What! Country is honour enough in all us – lordly head,
With heaven's lights high hung round, or, mother-ground
That mammocks, mighty foot. But no way sped,
Nor mind nor mainstrength; gold go garlanded
With, perilous, O nó; nor yet plod safe shod sound;
   Undenizened, beyond bound
Of earth's glory, earth's ease, all; no one, nowhere,
In wide the world's weal; rare gold, bold steel, bare
   In both; care, but share care –
This, by Despair, bred Hangdog dull; by Rage,
Manwolf, worse; and their packs infest the age.

Harry Ploughman

Hard as hurdle arms, with a broth of goldish flue
Breathed round; the rack of ribs; the scooped flank; lank
Rope-over thigh; knee-nave; and barrelled shank –
      Head and foot, shoulder and shank –
By a grey eye's heed steered well, one crew, fall to;
Stand at stress. Each limb's barrowy brawn, his thew
That onewhere curded, onewhere sucked or sank –
      Soared or sank –,
Though as a beechbole firm, finds his, as at a roll-call, rank
And features, in flesh, what deed he each must do –
      His sinew-service where do.

He leans to it, Harry bends, look. Back, elbow, and liquid waist
In him, all quail to the wallowing o' the plough:'s cheek crim-
   sons; curls
Wag or crossbridle, in a wind lifted, windlaced –
      See his wind- lilylocks -laced;
Churlsgrace, too, child of Amansstrength, how it hangs or hurls
Them – broad in bluffhide his frowning feet lashed! raced
With, along them, cragiron under and cold furls –
      With-a-fountain's shining-shot furls.

In Honour of St. Alphonsus Rodriguez
Laybrother of the Society of Jesus

Honour is flashed off exploit, so we say;
And those strokes once that gashed flesh or galled shield
Should tongue that time now, trumpet now that field,
And, on the fighter, forge his glorious day.
On Christ they do and on the martyr may;
But be the war within, the brand we wield
Unseen, the heroic breast not outward-steeled,
Earth hears no hurtle then from fiercest fray.

Yet God (that hews mountain and continent,
Earth, all, out; who, with trickling increment,
Veins violets and tall trees makes more and more)
Could crowd career with conquest while there went
Those years and years by of world without event
That in Majorca Alfonso watched the door.

That Nature is a Heraclitean Fire and of the comfort of the Resurrection

Cloud-puffball, torn tufts, tossed pillows | flaunt forth, then chevy
    on an air-
built thoroughfare: heaven-roysterers, in gay-gangs | they throng;
    they glitter in marches.
Down roughcast, down dazzling whitewash, | wherever an elm
    arches,
Shivelights and shadowtackle in long | lashes lace, lance, and pair.
Delightfully the bright wind boisterous | ropes, wrestles, beats earth
    bare
Of yestertempest's creases; in pool and rut peel parches
Squandering ooze to squeezed | dough, crust, dust; stanches,
    starches
Squadroned masks and manmarks | treadmire toil there
Footfretted in it. Million-fuelèd, | nature's bonfire burns on.
But quench her bonniest, dearest | to her, her clearest-selvèd spark
Man, how fast his firedint, | his mark on mind, is gone!
Both are in an unfathomable, all is in an enormous dark
Drowned. O pity and indig | nation! Manshape, that shone
Sheer off, disseveral, a star, | death blots black out; nor mark
       Is any of him at all so stark
But vastness blurs and time | beats level. Enough! the Resurrection,
A heart's-clarion! Away grief's gasping, | joyless days, dejection.
       Across my foundering deck shone
A beacon, an eternal beam. | Flesh fade, and mortal trash
Fall to the residuary worm; | world's wildfire, leave but ash:
       In a flash, at a trumpet crash,
I am all at once what Christ is, | since he was what I am, and
This Jack, joke, poor potsherd, | patch, matchwood, immortal
    diamond,
       Is immortal diamond.

Thou art indeed just, Lord, if I contend

Justus quidem tu es, Domine, si disputem tecum: verumtamen
justa loquar ad te: Quare via impiorum prosperatur? &c.[52]

Thou art indeed just, Lord, if I contend
With thee; but, sir, so what I plead is just.
Why do sinners' ways prosper? and why must
Disappointment all I endeavor end?

   Wert thou my enemy, O thou my friend,
How wouldst thou worse, I wonder, than thou dost
Defeat, thwart me? Oh, the sots and thralls of lust
Do in spare hours more thrive than I that spend,
Sir, life upon thy cause. See, banks and brakes
Now, leavèd how thick! lacèd they are again
With fretty chervil, look, and fresh wind shakes
Them; birds build – but not I build; no, but strain,
Time's eunuch, and not breed one work that wakes.
Mine, O thou lord of life, send my roots rain.

To R. B.

The fine delight that fathers thought; the strong
Spur, live and lancing like the blowpipe flame,
Breathes once and, quenchèd faster than it came,
Leaves yet the mind a mother of immortal song.
Nine months she then, nay years, nine years she long
Within her wears, bears, cares and moulds the same:
The widow of an insight lost she lives, with aim
Now known and hand at work now never wrong.

    Sweet fire the sire of muse, my soul needs this;
I want the one rapture of an inspiration.
O then if in my lagging lines you miss
The roll, the rise, the carol, the creation,
My winter world, that scarcely breathes that bliss
Now, yields you, with some sighs, our explanation.

Letters

(1884–1890)

Coventry Patmore was an English poet and literary critic, twenty-three years Hopkins's senior. He had also converted to Roman Catholicism, so the two shared a common language. But though Hopkins repeatedly tried to explain his sprung rhythm to Patmore, it seems the older man never grasped what Hopkins was striving for.

From Coventry Patmore, March 20, 1884

My Dear Mr. Hopkins, – I have read your poems – most of them several times – and find my first impression confirmed with each reading. It seems to me that the thought and feeling of these poems, if expressed without any obscuring novelty of mode, are such as often to require the whole attention to apprehend and digest them; and are therefore of a kind to appeal only to the few. But to the already sufficiently arduous character of such poetry you seem to me to have added the difficulty of following *several* entirely novel and simultaneous experiments in versification and construction, together with an altogether unprecedented system of alliteration and compound words; – any one of which novelties would be startling and productive of distraction from the poetic matter to be expressed.

System and learned theory are manifest in all these experiments; but they seem to me to be *too* manifest. To me they often darken the thought and feeling which all arts and artifices of language should only illustrate; and I often find it as hard to follow you as I have found it to follow the darkest parts of Browning – who, however, has not an equal excuse of philosophic system. . . . 'The Blessed Virgin compared to the Air we breathe' and a few other pieces are exquisite to my mind. . . . But I do not think that I could ever become sufficiently accustomed to your favorite poem, "The Wreck of the Deutschland" to reconcile me to its strangenesses. . . .

I should like to keep the MS. a little longer, and shall be very glad if you will allow me to copy two or three small pieces for my own use. But I will not do this unless you tell me I may.

Yours ever truly

C. Patmore

To A. W. M. Baillie, April 24, 1885, from Dublin

My Dearest Baillie, – I will this evening begin writing to you and God grant it may not be with this as it was with the last letter I wrote to an Oxford friend, that the should-be receiver was dead before it was ended. (There is no bad omen in this, as you will on reflexion – remark: REFLEXION: I used to write REFLECTION TILL YOU POINTED OUT THE MISTAKE; YOU DID SO TWICE, FOR! HAD, THROUGH HUMAN FRAILTY AND INADVERTENCE, lapsed – see.) I mean poor Geldart, whose death, as it was in Monday last's *Pall Mall,* you must have heard of. I suppose it was suicide, his mind, for he was a self-tormentor, having been unhinged, as it had been once or twice before, by a struggle he had gone through. Poor Nash's death, not long before, was certainly suicide and certainly too done in insanity, for he had been sleepless for ten nights: of this too you will have heard. It much comforts me and seems providential that I had renewed my friendship with Geldart some weeks before it was too late. I yesterday wrote to his widow. Three of my intimate friends at Oxford have thus drowned themselves, a good many more of my acquaintances and contemporaries have died by their own hands in other ways: it must be, and the fact brings it home to me, a dreadful feature of our days. . . .

May 8 – For one thing I was sorry when I got your late delightful letter. Since my sister told me of her meeting you I had been meaning to write and be first with you – but now I am slow even in answering. Some time since, I began to overhaul my old letters, accumulations of actually ever since I was at school, destroying all but a very few, and growing ever lother to destroy, but also to read, so that at last I left off reading; and there they lie and my old notebooks and beginnings of things, ever so many, which it seems to me might well have been done, ruins and wrecks; but on this theme I will not enlarge by pen and ink. . . .

To Robert Bridges, May 17, 1885, from Dublin

Dearest Bridges, – I must write something, though not so much as I have to say. The long delay was due to work, worry, and languishment of body and mind – which must be and will be; and indeed to diagnose my own case (for every man by forty is his own physician or a fool, they say; and yet again he who is his own physician has a fool for his patient – a form of epigram, by the bye, which, if you examine it, has a bad flaw), well then to judge of my case, I think that my fits of sadness, though they do not affect my judgment, resemble madness. Change is the only relief, and that I can seldom get. . . .

To R. W. Dixon, July 3, 1886

. . . But 'life is a short blanket' – profoundest of homely sayings: great gifts and great opportunities are more than life spares to one man. It is much if we get something, a spell, an innings at all. See how the great conquerors were cut short, Alexander, Caesar just seen[sic]. Above all Christ our Lord: his career was cut short and, whereas he would have wished to succeed by success – for it is insane to lay yourself out for failure, prudence is the first of the cardinal virtues, and he was the most prudent of men – nevertheless he was doomed to succeed by failure; his plans were baffled, his hopes dashed, and his work was done by being broken off undone. However much he understood all this he found it an intolerable grief to submit to it. He left the example: it is very strengthening, but except in that sense it is not consoling. . . .

To Robert Bridges, October 13, 1886

. . . Bye the bye, I say it deliberately and before God, I would have you and Canon Dixon and all true poets remember that fame, the being known, though in itself one of the most danger-ous things to man, is nevertheless the true and appointed air, element, and setting of genius and its works. What are the works of art for? to educate, to be standards. Education is meant for the many, standards are for public use. To produce then is of little use unless what we produce is known, if known widely known, the wider known the better, for it is by being known it works, it influences, it does its duty, it does good. We must then try to be known, aim at it, take means to it. And this without puffing in the process or pride in the success. But still. Besides, we are Englishmen. A great work by an Englishman is like a great battle won by England, it is an unfading bay tree. It will even be admired by and praised by and do good to those who hate England (as England is most perilously hated), who do not wish even to be benefited by her. It is then even a patriotic duty . . . to secure the fame and permanence of the work. Art and its fame do not really matter, spiritually they are nothing, virtue is the only good; but it is only by bringing in the infinite that to a just judgment they can be made to look infinitesimal or small or less than vastly great; and in this ordinary view of them I apply to them, and it is the true rule for dealing with them, what Christ our Lord said of virtue, Let your light shine before men that they may see your good works (say, of art) and glorify yr. Father in heaven (that is, acknowledge that they have an absolute excellence in them and are steps in a scale of infinite and inexhaustible excellence.)

To R. W. Dixon, December 1, 1888

(the very day 300 years ago of Father Campion's martyrdom)

My dear Friend,
. . . When a man has given himself to God's service, when he has denied himself and followed Christ, he has fitted himself to receive and does receive from God a special guidance, a more particular providence. This guidance is conveyed partly by the action of other men, as his appointed superiors, and partly by direct lights and inspirations. If I wait for such guidance, through whatever channel conveyed, about anything, about my

poetry for instance, I do more wisely in every way than if I try to serve my own seeming interests in the matter. Now if you value what I write, if I do myself, much more does our Lord. And if he chooses to avail himself of what I leave at his disposal he can do so with a felicity and with a success which I could never command. And if he does not, then two things follow: one, that the reward I shall nevertheless receive from him will be all the greater; the other, that then I shall know how much a thing contrary to his will and even to my own best interests I should have done if I had taken things into my own hands and forced on publication. This is my principle, and this in the main has been my practice: leading the sort of life I do here it seems easy, but when one mixes with the world and meets on every side its secret solicitations, to live by faith is harder, is very hard; nevertheless of God's help I shall always do so.

Our Society values, as you say, and has contributed to literature, to culture; but only as a means to an end. Its history and its experience show that literature proper, as poetry, has seldom been found to be to that end a very serviceable means. We have had for three centuries often the flower of the youth of a country in numbers enter our body: among these how many poets, how many artists of all sorts, there must have been! There have been very few Jesuit poets and, where they have been, I believe it would be found on examination that there was something exceptional in their circumstances or, so to say, counterbalancing in their career. For genius attracts fame, and individual fame St. Ignatius looked on as the most dangerous and dazzling of all attractions. . . .

You see then what is against me, but since, as Solomon says, there is a time for everything, there is nothing that does not some day come to be, it may be that the time will come for my verses. . . .

To His Mother, May 5, 1889, from Dublin

My dearest Mother, – I am grieved that you should be in such anxiety about me and I am afraid my letter to my father, which you must now have seen and ought, it seems to me, to have had before this morning's letter was sent, cannot much have relieved you. I am now in careful hands. The doctor thoroughly examined me yesterday. I have some fever; what, has not declared itself. I am to have perfect rest, and to take only liquid food. My pains and sleeplessness were due to suspended digestion, which has now been almost cured, but with much distress. There is no hesitation or difficulty about the nurses, with which Dublin is provided, I dare say, better than any place, but Dr. Redmond this morning said he must wait further to see the need: for today there is no real difference; only that I feel better.

You do not mention how Mary is.

I am, and I long have been, sad about Lionel, feeling that his visits must be few and far between and that I had so little good of this one, though he and I have so many interests in common and shd. find many more in company. I cd. not send him my Paper, for it had to be put aside.

It is an ill wind that blows nobody good. My sickness falling at the most pressing time of the University work, there will be the devil to pay. Only there is no harm in saying, that gives me no trouble but an unlooked for relief. At many such a time I have been in a sort of extremity of mind, now I am the placidest soul in the world. And you will see, when I come round, I shall be better for this.

I am writing uncomfortably and this is enough for a sick man. I am your loving son.

Best love to all.

Gerard

Letter from Charles Luxmoore to Hopkins's brother Arthur, June 13, 1890

My Dear Hopkins, –

I meant to have answered your letter before, and now I cannot for the moment lay my hands upon it, to see exactly what it was you said about your brother Gerard: but it was not my conception of him. I remember very well my first introduction to him, coming down the narrow staircase from Dyne's room with the ivth form, when as a new boy I had been put thro my paces, not without credit. Then as always I should have described 'Skin', as he was called, as one of the very best and nicest boys in the school, with his face always set to do what was right. When he was moved into our bedroom he was the only boy who regularly read to himself a small portion of the New Testament, in accordance I think with a promise given to his mother. At first it provoked a little ridicule, in which your brother must have got the best of us, tho' we didn't then think so, and I remember that my set decided that the promise was quite a sufficient reason, and we all agreed that Skin was not to be hindered in any way. I think this shows that your brother even at that time was both popular and respected. Tenacious when duty was concerned, he was full of fun, rippling over with jokes and chaff, facile with pencil and pen, with rhyming jibe or cartoon; good for his size at games and taking his part, but not as we did placing them first. Quiet, gentle, always nice, and always doing his work well. I think he must have been a charming boy from a master's point of view but he was completely changed by any wrong or ill treatment on their part. Once roused by a sense of undeserved injustice he, usually so quiet and docile, was furiously keen for the fray. . . . Then it was always an Homeric struggle to be fought inch by inch. A headmaster less heavy handed and headed than

Dyne would have appreciated the value of such a boy, and kept him ever on his side, but blustering Dyne's argument was always 'hold your tongue Sir', his firm conviction that a boy must be always wrong, and his appeal never to reason, always to force. Such a conflict was aroused by your brother's abstinence from all drink for three weeks, the pretext being a bet of 10 / to 6d, the real reason a conversation on seamen's sufferings and human powers of endurance. . . . Humanly speaking he made a grievous mistake in joining the Jesuits for on further acquaintance his whole soul must have revolted against a system which has killed many and many a noble soul; but what matters the means compared with the undoubted result. Any wood will do for the cross, when God's perfection is thereby reached. To get on with the Jesuits you must become on many grave points a machine, without will, without conscience, & that to this nature was an impossibility. To his lasting honour be it said he was too good for them, as he was for Dyne in his boyhood, and no earthly success could ever compare with the crown he has won and now wears. . . .

with every good wish I am your very truly

C. N. Luxmoore

Devotional Writings

(1883–1889)

Hopkins's journals and notebooks until this point had some struc-ture and coherence, but in Dublin he could not continue in an organized way. He held a double academic appointment: Pro-fessor of Classics at University College and Fellow of the Royal University of Ireland, and constantly felt overwhelmed. Leslie Higgins writes: "He felt assailed on every front: professional, voca-tional, spiritual, poetic. Not surprisingly, the strain and turmoil were also reflected in his personal note-taking." [53]

There were moments of inspiration, especially after each of his too few holidays in the country. But soon he would succumb to physical and mental exhaustion. Hopkins was diagnosed with typhoid, and could no longer grade the mountains of examina-tions that had become his nightmare. He lingered for three weeks, visited by friends and family. Paul Mariani speculates that Hop-kins's lifelong battle with diarrhea, hemorrhoids, and fatigue indicate that he suffered from Crohn's disease, which would not be named until 1932.

Whatever the case, Hopkins no longer had the stamina to fight the typhoid. Mariani depicts the end: "Around noon on Saturday, June 8 . . . with his mother and father there in the room with him, the dark waves finally wash over his bed and his fingers loosen and he slips quietly away. Earlier that day, Father Wheeler, making his rounds, has heard Gerard talking to himself. He comes closer to try and make out what he is saying. "I am so happy," he hears him whispering over and over. "I am so happy. I am so happy." [54]

In the following excerpts from his last journals, Hopkins openly confesses the burdens and triumphantly declares the joys that comprise the sum of his life.

Retreat in Ireland, 1889

January 1, 1888 [55] St. Stanislaus College, Tullabeg

Principium seu Fundamentum: 'Homo creatus est ut laudet' etc. – All moral good, all man's being good, lies in two things – in being right, being in the right, and in doing right; in being on the right side, on the side of good, and on that side of doing good. Neither of these will do by itself. Doing good but on the wrong side, promoting a bad cause, is rather doing wrong. Doing good but in no good cause is no merit: of whom or what does the doer deserve well? Not at any rate of God. Nor plainly is it enough to be on the right side and not promote it. . . .

But how is it with me? I was a Christian from birth or baptism, later I was converted to the Catholic faith and am enlisted twenty years in the Society of Jesus. I am now forty-four. I do not waver in my allegiance; I never had since my conversion to the Church. The question is how I advance the side I serve on. This may be inwardly or outwardly. Outwardly I often think I am employed to do what is of little or no use. . . .

I was continuing this train of thought this evening when I began to enter on that course of loathing and hopelessness which I have so often felt before, which made me fear madness and led me to give up the practice of meditation except, as now, in retreat and here it is again. I could therefore do no more than repeat *Justus es, Domine, et rectum judicium tuum*[56] and the like, and then being tired I nodded and woke with a start. What is my wretched life? Five wasted years almost have passed in Ireland. I am ashamed of the little I have done, of my waste of time, although my helplessness and weakness is such that I could scarcely do otherwise. And yet the Wise Man warns us against excusing ourselves in that fashion. I cannot then be excused; but what is life without aim, without spur, without help? All my undertakings miscarry: I am like a straining eunuch. I wish then for death: yet if I died now I should die imperfect, no master of myself, and that is the worst failure of all. O my God, look down on me.

January 2. This morning I made the meditation on the Three Sins, with nothing to enter but loathing of my life and a barren submission to God's will. The body cannot rest when it is in pain nor the mind be at peace as long as something bitter distills in it and it aches. This may be at any time and is at many: how then can it be pretended there is for those who feel this anything worth calling happiness in this world? There is a happiness, hope, the anticipation of happiness hereafter: it is better than happiness, but it is not happiness now. It is as if one were dazzled by a spark or star in the dark, seeing it but not seeing by it: we want a light shed on our way and a happiness spread over our life.

Afternoon: on the same – more loathing and only this thought, that I can do my spiritual and other duties better with God's help. In particular I think it may be well to resolve to make the examen every day at 1.15 and then say vespers and compline if not said before. I will consider what next.

January 3. Repetition of 1st and 2nd exercise – Helpless loathing. Then I went out and I said the *Te Deum*[57] and yet I thought what was needed was not praise of God but amendment of life.

January 5. Repetition of meditations on Incarnation and Nativity. . . .

But our lives and in particular those of religious, as mine, are in their whole direction, not only inwardly but most visibly and outwardly, shaped by Christ's. Without that even outwardly the world could be so different that we cannot even guess it. And my life is determined by the Incarnation down to most of the details of the day. Now this being so that I cannot even stop it, why should I not make the cause that determines my life, both as a whole and in much detail, determine it in greater detail still and to the greater efficiency of what I in any case should do, and to my greater happiness in doing it?

It is for this that St. Ignatius speaks of the angel *discharging his mission,* it being a question of action leading up to, as now my action leads from, the Incarnation. The Incarnation was for my salvation and that of the world: the work goes on in a great system and machinery which even drags me on with the collar round my neck though I could and do neglect my duty in it. But I say to myself that I am only too willing to do God's work and help on the knowledge of the Incarnation. But this is not really true: I am not willing enough for the piece of work assigned me, the only work I am given to do, though I could do others if they were given. This is my work at Stephen's Green. And I thought that the Royal University was to me what Augustus's enrolment was to St. Joseph: *exiit sermo a Caesare Augusto,*[58] etc.; so resolution of the senate of the R.U. came to me, inconvenient and painful, but the journey to Bethlehem was inconvenient and painful; and then I am bound in justice, and paid. I hope to bear this in mind.

Instructions: The Principle or Foundation

Homo creatus est – CREATION THE MAKING OUT OF NOTHING, bringing from nothing into being: once there was nothing, then lo, this huge world was there. How great a work of power!

The loaf is made with flour; the house with bricks; the plough, the cannon, the locomotive, the warship / of iron – all of things that were before, of matter; but the world, with the flour, the grain, the wheatear, the seed, the ground, the sun, the rain; with the bricks, the clay, the earth; with the iron and the mine, the fuel and the furnace, was made from nothing. And they are MADE IN TIME AND WITH LABOUR, the world in no time with a word. MAN CANNOT CREATE a single speck, God creates all that is besides himself.

But MEN OF GENIUS ARE SAID TO CREATE a painting, a poem, a tale, a tune, a policy; not indeed the colours and the canvas, not the words or notes, but the design, the character, the air, the plan. How then? – from themselves, from their own minds. And they themselves, their minds and all, are creatures of God: if the tree created much more the flower and the fruit. . . .

WHY DID GOD CREATE? – Not for sport, not for nothing. Every sensible man has a purpose in all he does, every workman has a use for every object he makes. Much more has God a purpose, an end, a meaning in his work. He meant the world to give him praise, reverence, and service: to give him glory. It is like a garden, a field he sows: what should it bear him? Praise, reverence, and service; it should yield him glory. It is an estate he farms: what should it bring him in? Praise, reverence, and service; it should repay him glory. It is a leasehold he lets out:

what should its rent be? Praise, reverence, and service; its rent is his glory. It is a bird he teaches to sing, a pipe, a harp he plays on: what should it sing to him? etc. It is a glass he looks in: what should it shew him? With praise, reverence, and service it should shew him his own glory. It is a book he has written, of the riches of his knowledge, teaching endless truths, full lessons of wisdom, a poem of beauty: what is it about? His praise, the reverence due to him, the way to serve him; it tells him of his glory. It is a censer fuming: what is the sweet incense? His praise, his reverence, his service; it rises to his glory. It is an altar and a victim lying in his sight: why is it offered? To his praise, honour, and service: it is a sacrifice to his glory. . . .

But AMIDST THEM ALL IS MAN, man and the angels: we will speak of man. Man was created. Like the rest then to praise, reverence and serve God; to give him glory. He does so, even by his being, beyond all visible creatures: 'What a piece of work is man!'. . . . But man can know God, *can mean to give him glory.* This then was why he was made, to give God glory and to mean to give it; to praise God fréely, wíllingly to reverence him, gládly to serve him. Man was made to give, and mean to give, God glory.

I WAS MADE FOR THIS, each one of us was made for this.

A CHRONOLOGY

1844

+ *July 28:* Born at Stratford, Essex, eldest son of Manley and Catherine Smith Hopkins; he will have eight younger siblings

1845

+ *October:* John Henry Newman resigns his fellowship at Oriel College, Oxford, and joins the Roman Catholic Church

1847

+ *May 30:* Newman is ordained a Roman Catholic priest

1850

+ *April 23:* William Wordsworth dies and Tennyson is appointed poet laureate of England
+ *September 29:* Pope Pius IX re-establishes, for the first time since the Protestant Reformation of the mid-sixteenth century, a Roman Catholic Cardinal (Henry Manning) in England

1852

+ The Hopkins family moves to Oak Hill, Hampstead, London

1854

+ Hopkins Attends Cholmeley Grammar School, referred to as Highgate, London, under Headmaster Dyne

1859

+ Hopkins wins Highgate prize for his poem "The Escorial"
+ Darwin publishes *On the Origin of Species*

1862

+ Hopkins wins another Highgate prize for his poem "A Vision of the Mermaids"

+ Wins the Governors' Gold Medal for Latin Verse and a Highgate Exhibition (a scholarship)

1863

+ *January:* Hopkins wins scholarship to Balliol, Oxford

+ *Easter:* Sits his final exams at Highgate

+ *April:* Hopkins comes up to Oxford, meets what will become his long-term friends Bridges, Geldart, and Addis; attends Canon Henry Parry Liddon's lectures on Tractarianism

1864

+ *February 2:* Hopkins first goes to confession to Liddon

+ Writes many poems including "Barnfloor and Winepress," "Heaven-Haven," and "St. Dorothea"

+ Wins a First in Mods (the Oxford course in Greek and Latin literature)

+ Newman publishes *Apologia pro Vita Sua*

1865

+ *March:* Hopkins undergoes religious crisis

+ Goes to confession to Dr. Pusey

+ Newman publishes *Dream of Gerontius*

1866

+ Hopkins writes numerous poems including "Habit of Perfection" and "Nondum"

- *April:* Begins to study with Walter Pater

- *June:* With his friend Addis, goes to Benedictine Monastery

- *July 16–18:* Decides to become Roman Catholic

- *September 20:* Consults Father Newman in Birmingham

- *October 21:* Newman receives Hopkins into the Roman Catholic Church

- *November 4:* Hopkins confirmed by Archbishop Manning

1867

- Hopkins graduates from Oxford with a Double-First

- Benjamin Jowett calls him "Star of Balliol"

- Hopkins becomes a teacher of Classics at the Oratory School, Birmingham

1868

- *February 9:* Hopkins first uses the term "inscape" in his notebook

- *May:* Decides to become a priest, burns his poems

- *September 7:* Enters the Jesuit novitiate at Manresa House, in Roehampton, a suburb of southwest London, for two years of training

- *September 16:* Begins his first Long (Thirty-Day) Retreat

- *November 17:* Preaches his first sermon, on the feast of St. Stanislaus

1869

- *July 28:* Hopkins turns twenty-five

- *December:* Serves as porter of the college until February 1870, entering notes in the daily log of events

1870

- *July 18:* Pope Pius IX declares papal infallibility during the First Vatican Council
- *September 8:* Hopkins takes First Vows as a Jesuit, and begins to wear a gown, biretta, and Roman collar
- *September 9:* Begins as a Jesuit Scholastic to study the philosophate at St. Mary's Hall, Stonyhurst, Lancashire

1871

- *July:* Hopkins sits for the first-year examinations in philosophy

1872

- *May 22:* Hopkins visits the observatory to watch a lunar eclipse
- *December 30:* Has surgery for hemorrhoids while home with his family for Christmas
- Addis, Wood, Bond, and Baillie visit him

1873

- Hopkins returns to Roehampton to teach Classics to Jesuit "juniors"
- Makes notes on prosody
- *June 23:* Takes examinations in philosophy
- *September 9:* Starts teaching rhetoric at Roehampton

1874

- *August 28:* Hopkins begins theologate at St. Beuno's College in North Wales
- Resumes correspondence with Oxford friend Robert Bridges
- *September 19:* Hopkins takes minor orders (doorkeeper, reader, exorcist, acolyte)

+ *October 8:* Visits St. Winefred's Well (now called St. Winefride's Well) in Holywell, Flintshire, Wales

1875

+ *December:* "The Wreck of the Deutschland"

+ Hopkins resumes writing poetry

1876

+ Sends "The Wreck of the Deutschland" to Jesuit magazine *The Month,* which ultimately rejects it

1877

+ *February–September:* Hopkins writes ten sonnets

+ *March 3:* Passes moral theology exam and can hear confessions

+ *March 11:* Preaches a practice Sunday sermon ("Make the men sit down") and congregation laughs

+ *September 23:* Ordained a priest at St. Beuno's

1878

+ *April:* Hopkins starts to teach at Stonyhurst College, preparing pupils for exams at the University of London

+ *June:* Begins to correspond with Canon Richard Watson Dixon

+ *July–November:* Acting curate at Mount Street, London

+ *August:* Begins preaching at Farm Street, London

+ *December:* Moves to Oxford as curate at St. Aloysius

+ Renews relationship with Walter Pater, his former tutor, and with Francis and Frances Paravicini (The Baron Francis de Paravicini was a classmate of Hopkins at Oxford)

1879

+ Hopkins composes nine poems
+ *July–September:* Preaches at Oxford
+ *October–December:* Preaches at Bedford Leigh

1880

+ *January:* Hopkins becomes preacher at St. Francis Xavier's, Liverpool, among Irish immigrants – stays almost two years
+ Writes "Inversnaid," "Spring and Fall"

1881

+ Hopkins writes "Felix Randal"
+ *August 10:* Serves as curate in Glasgow for seven weeks
+ *October 10:* Begins tertianship (third year of novitiate) at Manresa House, Roehampton
+ *November 7–December 8:* Long Retreat
+ Writes partial commentary on *The Spiritual Exercises of St. Ignatius*
+ Produces most of his spiritual writing

1882

+ Hopkins writes "The Leaden Echo and the Golden Echo" and "Ribblesdale"
+ *May–July:* Bridges visits Hopkins three times
+ *August 15:* Hopkins completes tertianship and takes Final Vows as a Jesuit
+ *August 31:* Moves to Stonyhurst to teach Latin and Greek

1883

+ Hopkins writes "The Blessed Virgin Compared with the Air We Breathe"

+ Begins correspondence with Coventry Patmore, a poet twenty years his senior

+ *August 26–27:* The volcano Krakatoa erupts in Indonesia

+ *November 15:* Hopkins publishes letter in *Nature* magazine about the impact of Krakatoa, and will publish three more letters in *Nature* between December 1883 and October 1884

1884

+ *January 30:* Hopkins appointed Fellow of University College in Dublin, the Catholic College founded by John Henry Newman, to teach Latin and Greek, and receives a fellowship at the Royal University of Ireland

+ *February 18:* Moves to 85–86 St. Stephen's Green in Dublin

+ *September–October:* Overwhelmed and exhausted by setting and grading examination papers in Latin grammar, translation, and composition, and in advanced Greek composition

+ *November:* Writes "Spelt from Sybil's Leaves"

1885

+ Hopkins writes the "terrible sonnets"

1886

+ *March–April:* significant correspondence with Oxford classmate A. W. M. Baillie

+ *May:* Hopkins visits Robert Bridges in England

+ *November:* Meets William Butler Yeats

1887

+ Hopkins writes "Harry Ploughman" and "Tom's Garland"
+ *February:* Third anniversary of his moving to Dublin, which he has found "three hard wearying wasting wasted years"
+ *August:* Takes vacation in England and visits Baillie and Bridges

1888

+ Hopkins writes "That Nature is a Heraclitean Fire" and "In Honour of St. Alphonsus Rodriguez"
+ *July 28:* His forty-fourth, and last, birthday

1889

+ *January 1–6:* Makes retreat at St. Stanislaus College, Tullabeg
+ Hopkins writes "Thou art indeed just, Lord" and "To R. B."
+ *April:* Francis de Paravicini visits Hopkins in Dublin; describes him as looking very ill
+ *May 6:* Hopkins tells his parents he has "a sort of typhoid"
+ *June 5:* His parents arrive at his bedside
+ *June 8:* Hopkins dies of typhoid fever and peritonitis
+ Buried in Catholic cemetery Glasnevin

ENDNOTES

Part I

1. Humphry House, *The Note-Books and Papers of Gerard Manley Hopkins* (Oxford: Oxford University Press, 1937), 416.

2. Graham Storey, *A Preface to Hopkins* (New York: Longman, 1981), 12.

3. Ibid., 11.

4. Hopkins's obituary in *Letters and Notices*, xx (1889–90): 175–6.

5. Claude Colleer Abbott, ed., *Further Letters of Gerard Manley Hopkins, including his Correspondence with Coventry Patmore* (Oxford: Oxford University Press, 1938), 435.

6. M. C. D'Arcy, *Archivum Historicum Societas Jesu* I, 1, (January–March 1932), 118–22.

Part II

7. Leslie Higgins, ed., *Gerard Manley Hopkins: Diaries, Journals, and Notebooks* III (Oxford: Oxford University Press, 2015), 15–16.

8. Evelyn Waugh, "Come Inside," in *The Road to Damascus*, ed. John A. O'Brien (Garden City, NY: Doubleday, 1949), 15–20.

9. Norman White, *Hopkins: A Literary Biography* (Oxford: Clarendon Press, 1992), 80.

10. Higgins, *Diaries, Journals, and Notebooks*, 2–3.

11. "Enoch Arden": poem by Tennyson published in 1864.

12. "Composed Near Calais, on the Road Leading to Ardres, August 7, 1902": poem by William Wordsworth.

13. Catherine Phillips, ed., *Gerard Manley Hopkins: The Major Works* (Oxford: Oxford University Press, 1986, 2002), xx–xxi.

14. Psalm 125:1: "They that trust in the Lord shall be as Mount Zion."

15. John Duns Scotus (c. 1265–1308), *Commentary on the Four Sentences of Peter Lombard*.

16. Baddely: misspelling of Edward Badeley, who bequeathed a generous collection of books to Stonyhurst College in 1868.

Part III

17. W. H. Gardner, ed., *Gerard Manley Hopkins: Poems and Prose* (Harmondsworth, UK: Penguin Books, 1963), xiv.

18. White, *Literary Biography,* 256.

19. J. Hillis Miller, *The Linguistic Moment* (Princeton, NJ: Princeton University Press, 1985), 252–3.

20. Helen Vendler, *The Breaking of Style* (Cambridge, MA: Harvard University Press, 1995), 15.

21. Miller, *The Linguistic Moment,* 245–7.

22. The Falk Laws of 1873–1875 were enacted in the German Kingdom of Prussia during the Kulturkampf conflict with the Catholic Church. Jesuits were expelled in 1873, and other orders associated with them, such as the Nuns of the Sacred Heart, were expelled in 1874. The nuns commemorated in "The Wreck of the Deutschland" were Franciscans.

23. The Bremen Stanza: stanza 12 of Hopkins's poem, "The Wreck of the Deutschland."

24. John Milton, *Lycidas,* lines 70–72.

25. John Milton, *Paradise Regained,* book IV, line 638.

26. Ibid., book I, line 175.

Part IV

27. Paul Mariani, *Gerard Manley Hopkins: A Life* (New York: Viking, 2008), 181.

28. Alfred Thomas, "Hopkins's 'Felix Randal': the Man and the Poem," *Times Literary Supplement,* (March 19, 1971), 331–2.

29. J. Hillis Miller, *The Disappearance of God* (Cambridge, MA: Belknap Press of Harvard University, 1975).

30. William Wordsworth, Preface to *Lyrical Ballads* (London: T. N. Longman and O. Rees, 1800), xxxiii.

31. Christopher Devlin, SJ, ed., *The Sermons and Devotional Writings of Gerard Manley Hopkins* (Oxford: Oxford University Press, 1959), xiii.

32. A.M.D.G. – *Ad Majoram Dei Gloria:* for the greater glory of God.

33. John 8:12: "I am the light of the world. Whoever follows me will not walk in darkness, but will have the light of life."

34. Devlin, *Sermons,* 5.

35. Ibid., 107–9.

36. Paul Mariani, "Towards a Poetics of Unselfconsciousness." *Renascence* 29, Issue 1 (Autumn 1976), 43–49.

Part V

37. Phillips, *Major Works,* xxxiii.

38. Norman White, *Hopkins in Ireland* (Dublin: University College Dublin Press, 2002), 15.

39. Ibid., 365.

40. Ibid., 17.

41. Ibid., 16.

42. Ibid., 17.

43. *Dies Irae* (Day of Wrath): a medieval Latin hymn about the Day of Judgment sung in requiem masses.

44. White, *Literary Biography*, vii.

45. Ibid.

46. Ibid., 332.

47. White, *Literary Biography*, 332.

48. René Gallet, "Gerard Manley Hopkins as a Metaphysical Poet," *Hopkins Quarterly* 26, no. 3–4 (Summer–Fall 1999): 67, 68.

49. Brad Leithauser, "Comforting Talk," *The New Yorker* (May 20, 2014).

50. White, *Literary Biography*, vi.

51. Phillip Endean, SJ, "The Spirituality of Gerard Manley Hopkins," *Hopkins Quarterly* VIII, no. 3 (Fall 1981), 126–129.

52. Jeremiah 12:1: "Thou, indeed, O Lord, art just, if I plead with thee, but yet I will speak what is just to thee: Why doth the way of the wicked prosper?"

53. Higgins, *Diaries, Journals, and Notebooks*, 10.

54. Mariani, *Gerard Manley Hopkins*, 425.

55. Christopher Devlin, SJ, editor of *The Sermons and Devotional Writings of Gerard Manley Hopkins*, claims that Hopkins made this retreat in January 1888; Norman White in *Hopkins: A Literary Biography* claims it was January 1889. Lesley Higgins and Michael F. Suarez, SJ, editors of *The Dublin Notebook*. Vol. VII, *The Collected Works of Gerard Manley Hopkins*, point out that the retreat occurred January 1–6, 1889, and "1888" was Hopkins's own misprint of the date.

56. Ps. 119:137: "Thou art just, O Lord, and thy judgment is right."

57. *Te Deum:* An early Christian hymn of praise. The first words are *Te Deum laudamus*, "Thee, O God, we praise."

58. Luke 2:1: ". . . there went forth a decree from Caesar Augustus."

SELECTED BIBLIOGRAPHY

Abbott, Claude Colleer, ed. *Further Letters of Gerard Manley Hopkins, including his Correspondence with Coventry Patmore.* Oxford: Oxford University Press, 1938.

Bridges, Robert, ed. *Poems of Gerard Manley Hopkins: Edited with Notes by Robert Bridges.* London: Oxford University Press, 1930, 1944.

Devlin, Christopher, SJ, ed. *The Sermons and Devotional Writings of Gerard Manley Hopkins.* Oxford: Oxford University Press, 1959.

Endean, Philip, SJ. "The Spirituality of Gerard Manley Hopkins" *Hopkins Quarterly* VIII, no. 3, (Fall 1981).

Gardner, W. H., ed. *Gerard Manley Hopkins: Poems and Prose.* Harmondsworth, UK: Penguin Books, 1963.

Gardner, W. H. and N. H. MacKenzie, eds. *The Poems of Gerard Manley Hopkins,* 4th ed. London: Oxford University Press, 1970.

Higgins, Leslie, ed. Vol III, *Gerard Manley Hopkins: Diaries, Journals, and Notebooks.* Oxford: Oxford University Press, 2015.

House, Humphry. *The Note-Books and Papers of Gerard Manley Hopkins.* Oxford: Oxford University Press, 1937.

House, Humphry and Graham Storey, eds. *Journals and Papers of Gerard Manley Hopkins.* Oxford: Oxford University Press, 1959.

Mariani, Paul. *Gerard Manley Hopkins: A Life.* New York: Viking, 2008.

_____ . "Towards a Poetics of Unselfconsciousness." *Renascence* 29, Issue 1 (Autumn 1976): 43–49.

Miller, J. Hillis. *The Linguistic Moment.* Princeton, NJ: Princeton University Press, 1985.

Phillips, Catherine, ed. *Gerard Manley Hopkins: The Major Works.* Oxford: Oxford University Press, 1986, 2002.

Storey, Graham. *A Preface to Hopkins.* New York: Longman, 1981.

Vendler, Helen. *The Breaking of Style.* Cambridge, MA: Harvard University Press, 1995.

White, Norman. *Hopkins: A Literary Biography.* Oxford: Clarendon Press, 1992.

_____ . *Hopkins in Ireland.* Dublin: University College Dublin Press, 2002.

INDEX OF TITLES AND FIRST LINES

Titles in italics

OTHER TITLES FROM PLOUGH

The Gospel in Dostoyevsky: Selections from His Works. Passages from Dostoyevsky's greatest novels explore the devastating, yet ultimately healing, implications of the Gospels.

The Gospel in Tolstoy: Selections from His Short Stories, Spiritual Writings, and Novels. A rich, accessible introduction to one of the world's greatest novelists, this anthology shows how the life and teachings of Jesus inspired some of Tolstoy's best literary work.

The Gospel in George MacDonald: Selections from His Novels, Fairy Tales, and Spiritual Writings. Discover the spiritual vision of the great Scottish storyteller who inspired C. S. Lewis and J. R. R. Tolkien.

Provocations: The Spiritual Writings of Kierkegaard. Introduces a man whose writings pare away the fluff of modern spirituality to reveal the basics of the Christ-centered life: decisiveness, obedience, and recognition of the truth.

Salt and Light: Living the Sermon on the Mount by Eberhard Arnold. Unlike dozens of other books on the "Great Teaching" of Jesus, this one not only interprets it, but also says that it ought to be put into practice.

My God and My All: The Life of Saint Francis of Assisi by Elizabeth Goudge. The ever-fascinating life of Saint Francis, retold for today's readers by one of the great novelists of our time.

Plough Publishing House
www.plough.com
PO BOX 398, Walden, NY 12586, USA
Robertsbridge, East Sussex TN32 5DR, UK
4188 Gwydir Highway, Elsmore, NSW 2360, AU